This book belongs to

The ornament of a house is the Friends who frequent it. — RALPH WALDO EMERSON

Book 5

Content and Artwork by **Gooseberry Patch Company**

**LEISURE ARTS**
**Vice President and Editor-in-Chief:** Sandra Graham Case
**Executive Director of Publications:** Cheryl Nodine Gunnells
**Director of Designer Relations:** Debra Nettles
**Publications Director:** Kristine Anderson Mertes
**Design Director:** Cyndi Hansen
**Editorial Director:** Susan Frantz Wiles
**Photography Director:** Lori Ringwood Dimond
**Art Operations Director:** Jeff Curtis
**Director of Public Relations and Retail Marketing:** Stephen Wilson
**Licensed Product Coordinator:** Lisa Truxton Curton

**EDITORIAL STAFF**

**EDITORIAL**
**Managing Editor:** Alan Caudle
**Senior Editor:** Linda L. Garner

**TECHNICAL**
**Managing Editor:** Leslie Schick Gorrell
**Book Coordinator and Senior Technical Writer:** Theresa Hicks Young
**Technical Writers:** Christina Price Kirkendoll and Shawnna B. Manes
**Technical Associate:** Lois Long

**FOODS**
**Foods Editor:** Celia Fahr Harkey, R.D.
**Technical Assistant:** Judy Millard

**OXMOOR HOUSE**
**Editor-in-Chief:** Nancy Fitzpatrick Wyatt
**Executive Editor:** Susan Carlisle Payne
**Editor:** Kelly Hooper Troiano
**Photographers:** Jim Bathie and Brit Huckabay
**Contributing Photo Stylists:** Connie Formby and Katie Stoddard
**Test Kitchen Director:** Elizabeth Tyler Luckett
**Test Kitchen Assistant Director:** Julie Christopher
**Recipe Editor:** Gayle Hays Sadler
**Test Kitchen Staff:** Kristi Carter, Nicole L. Faber, Kathleen Royal Phillips, Jan A. Smith, Elise Weiss and Kelley Self Wilton

**DESIGN**
**Design Manager:** Diana Sanders Cates
**Design Captains:** Anne Pulliam Stocks and Becky Werle
**Designers:** Cherece Athy, Polly Tullis Browning, Peggy Elliott Cunningham and Linda Diehl Tiano
**Craft Assistant:** Lucy Combs Beaudry

**ART**
**Art Publications Director:** Rhonda Shelby
**Art Imaging Director:** Mark Hawkins
**Art Category Manager:** Lora Puls
**Lead Graphic Artist:** Mark Potter
**Graphic Artists:** Dayle Cosh, Rebecca Hester, Dana Vaughn and Elaine Wheat
**Photographer:** Russell Ganser
**Photo Stylists:** Janna Laughlin and Cassie Newsome
**Publishing Systems Administrator:** Becky Riddle
**Publishing Systems Assistants:** Clint Hanson, Myra S. Means and Chris Wertenberger

**PROMOTIONS**
**Associate Editor:** Steven M. Cooper
**Designer:** Dale Rowett
**Graphic Artists:** Teresa Boyd and Deborah Kelly

**BUSINESS STAFF**
**Publisher:** Rick Barton
**Vice President, Finance:** Tom Siebenmorgen
**Director of Corporate Planning and Development:** Laticia Mull Dittrich
**Vice President, Retail Marketing:** Bob Humphrey
**Vice President, Sales:** Ray Shelgosh
**Vice President, National Accounts:** Pam Stebbins
**Director of Sales and Services:** Margaret Reinold
**Vice President, Operations:** Jim Dittrich
**Comptroller, Operations:** Rob Thieme
**Retail Customer Service Managers:** Sharon Hall and Stan Raynor
**Print Production Manager:** Fred F. Pruss

Library of Congress Catalog Number 99-71586
Hardcover ISBN 1-57486-273-1
Softcover ISBN 1-57486-274-X

10   9   8   7   6   5   4   3   2   1

# Christmas

## Book 5

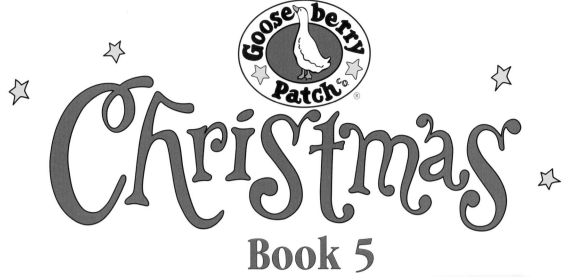

A LEISURE ARTS PUBLICATION

# Christmas

## Gooseberry Patch

*For all our Gooseberry Patch friends &
family...wishing you joyful holiday memories!*

# How Did Gooseberry Patch Get Started?

**Y**ou may know the story of Gooseberry Patch...the tale of two country friends who decided one day over the backyard fence to try their hands at the mail order business. Started in JoAnn's kitchen back in 1984, Vickie & JoAnn's dream of a "Country Store in Your Mailbox" has grown and grown to a 96-page catalog with over 400 products, including cookie cutters, Santas, snowmen, gift baskets, angels and our very own line of cookbooks! What an adventure for two country friends!

**T**hrough our catalogs and books, Gooseberry Patch has met country friends from all over the world. While sharing letters and phone calls, we found that our friends love to cook, decorate, garden and craft. We've created Kate, Holly & Mary Elizabeth to represent these devoted friends who live and love the country lifestyle the way we do. They're just like you & me... they're our "Country Friends®!"

*Your friends at Gooseberry Patch*

Mary Elizabeth * Holly * Kate * Spot

# Contents

## All Through the House

COUNTRY · FRIEND · IDEAS · FOR · CHRISTMAS

# Wrap Up the Holidays .........................54

# Goodies for Giving .........................72

# Festive Fare.........................86

# Christmas Memories

Each year, we look forward to decorating for the holidays. As we pull boxes of memories from the attic and carefully unpack each one, our hearts return to those fun-filled Christmases of childhood. It's the little things we recall so vividly…the aroma from Mom's kitchen as she removed a pan of cookies from the oven, the comfort of snuggling beneath Grandma's best quilt, the thrill of being lifted high in Daddy's arms to place a tinsel star atop the tree. As you turn the pages, you'll discover unique ways to preserve treasured memories, and create new ones, too!

*Make a memory wreath to display your family's holiday heirlooms…those lovely glass balls that are too fragile to be placed within reach of little ones, the one-of-a-kind ornaments and copies of cherished photos. Simply arrange the items on an evergreen wreath, then either wire or glue them in place!*

8

# You Better Watch Out!

DEC. 23

NAUGHTY OR NICE?

*You won't believe how easy it is to design a personalized family photo calendar…the hardest part will be deciding on the snapshots! Instructions for the flip photo calendar are on page 120.*

Bundle up the kids and take a ride to enjoy all the holiday lights…the kids can even wear their pajamas! Wrap up in cozy blankets, sing carols and enjoy a fun-filled evening together.

*"Remembered joys are never past."*

— James Montgomery

Invite your mother, grandmother and the rest of your family to bring their family albums and boxes of photographs to your Thanksgiving gathering. After dinner, you can sort through family photos…jot down dates and locations, add remembrances of the different occasions and identify any "mystery relatives." You'll be ready to start your own family album in no time!

On December 1st, I put a little stuffed elf somewhere in the house. He watches to see who is naughty or nice. Each morning he is in a different place. Then, on December 24th, he disappears to report to Santa, not to be seen again until next December 1st. My children are all grown now, and still the elf watches.

— Marlaine Pietrzak

My mother always kept a Holiday Journal. It included a passage from each family member, in which we reflected on the year in passing and discussed our dreams for the New Year. She also listed all the Christmas presents we received and included a snapshot taken on Christmas morning each year. Now our Holiday Journal is a part of our family history, and we only wish we had five copies! However, I have started my own journal.

— Maureen George

*"Cherish all your happy moments… they make a fine cushion for old age."*

— Ramona Mullins

Our family has been keeping a "Holiday Memory" photo book of all our Christmas parties and dinners for over 25 years. The children and grandchildren love to page through all the memories of good times shared…a wonderful legacy to pass on.

— Kristin Ammermann

*"The best things in life are not free but priceless."*

— Benjamin Lichtenberg

I am lucky enough to have the sled my husband played on when he was a child. All of his older brothers also played with it, and the oldest brother is 89 years old! At Christmas, I stand the sled by the front door, tie a spray of greenery with a red bow to the front of the sled and then hang a pair of antique skates.

— Norma Longnecker
Lawrenceville, IL

On a wintry afternoon, my mother decided to spend her hibernation time cleaning out a box of ancient paperwork. When she's done this in the past, I've received immunization records and other medical documents, as Mom attempts to empty her attic and fill mine. So it was no surprise when an envelope arrived in the mail with a funny notation on the exterior flap that read, "You began wearing glasses on 11/27/62." (I was 4$^1$/$_2$ at the time.) I chuckled at the thought that Mom was now sending me all of my records from the optician. I opened the envelope and, to my surprise, I held in my hand various sizes of scrap paper. The year was written at the top of each piece of paper, and beneath the year was a list detailing each Christmas gift my parents purchased for me, from the year I was born to present. Also included were letters I wrote to Santa as a child. My eyes filled with tears at this simple, but precious, loving act of my mother, who took the time to compile, preserve and share these lasting memories. I thank God daily for the special relationship I share with my family. While miles may separate us now, our caring hearts will remain forever close!

— Wendy Posavec
Gerbauer

*While your children are little, start collecting keepsakes to fill a shadowbox for each one. Pictures with Santa, favorite toys, handwritten notes and "1st" ornaments are all wonderful memories; just arrange & glue in place.*

Once your children are old enough to come up with "wish lists" for Christmas, date them and file away after Santa has done his shopping. When your children are grown, they will enjoy looking over a piece of their past.

— Beverly Botten

*These nostalgic frames are the perfect settings for old family photos! To make them, embellish inexpensive paper frames*

Our big family has always been very close. Christmas was the day we all gathered at my grandparents' house. After I married, we moved 1,500 miles away. I missed my family terribly. One year my husband had a business trip near my grandparents' city. He went to their house for the annual holiday get-together. When he got ready to leave, Grandma reached up high on their Christmas tree and took off an old glass bird ornament with a feathered brush tail. It had hung on their tree for as long as I could remember. She sent it home with him for me. Many years have since passed, but each year I take the lovely old bird from its box and reverently place it on our Christmas tree. Someday it will be passed on to one of my daughters, who will love it and cherish it as much as I have.

— Nancy Campbell
Bellingham, WA

Decorate your tree with your children's outgrown mittens, baby socks and booties for a darling memory tree. A tiny bonnet or stocking cap will make a sweet tree topper!

A few years ago, my husband's grandmother gave our family hand-knitted stockings. Although we didn't have a fireplace to hang them on, I bought an old mantel to decorate. After lots of scraping and a couple of coats of paint, it was ready. On our new mantel, I placed a garland with white lights, red pillar candles in hurricane lamps, my snowman collection and, of course, our stockings. It was very pretty...and so much fun for our sons to find their stockings on the mantel Christmas morning!

— Michelle Corder
Alvaton, KY

*with stamped designs, vellum and other trims. Complete instructions for the frame garland are on page 120.*

Early into my marriage, over 30 years ago, I learned that becoming a military family meant constantly making new friends and saying goodbye to old ones. I wanted to remember those friends for years to come, so I designed a holiday memory tree. As the holiday parties began, families invited to our home were asked to bring one favorite ornament. As each guest arrived, I would write their name and the date on the ornament. I explained that each ornament on the tree held a special memory of friendship, and that each family who brought an ornament to share could choose an ornament of ours from the tree to take home with them as a reminder of the evening. Each year it was so much fun to open the memory box of ornaments and to remember our friends, wherever they were.

— Leekay Bennett
Delaware, OH

Coming from a big family, Christmas has always meant getting together with dozens of relatives and going to Grandma Teuscher's for Christmas Eve dinner. My favorite Christmas memory is the year a big windstorm hit our town and the power went out. After lighting candles, we all gathered in front of the fire, and each of us shared our favorite Christmas memories. That night there were four generations laughing and crying together about Christmases past…I will never forget the closeness we felt.

— Rachel Keller
Bothell, WA

"Christmas is not in tinsel and lights…it's lighting a fire inside the heart."

— Wilfred A. Peterson

# Recall it as often as you wish...

JOY
MERRY CHRISTMAS!
2003
LOVE
FAMILY TRADITIONS

WONDERFUL
BAKER
QUILTER
ARTIST
GRANDMA
GENTLE
WARM

SENSITIVE
ATHLETIC
CUTE
CHARMING
MATT
MAKES YOU LAUGH!

## ...A happy memory never wears out.

—LIBBIE FUDIM

VICKIE

*Oh, what fun you'll have crafting this whimsical "family tree"! The wooden dowel tree is simple to paint and assemble, then decorate with personalized gift-tag ornaments. See page 120 for the nametag family tree how-to's.*

# Sparkles and Wishes

A big wreath for the front door, garlands and ornaments ready to place on the tree, stockings to hang by the chimney with care...Kate, Holly & Mary Elizabeth are all set to decorate for the holidays! No matter what your style, you'll find plenty of Christmas trims to add to your collection, from homespun snowmen to shiny bells and old-fashioned gingerbread cut-outs. There's even an ornament-crafting party to throw for your friends. Get ready, get set...let's deck the halls!

*Don't wait until Christmas Eve to hang these stockings! Trimmed with homespun appliqués and buttons, they're perfect for filling with goodies. Turn to page 120 for the flannel stocking how-to's.*

*Invite one and all to an ornament-making party early in December, and help your friends get a head start on their handcrafted tree-trims! For stress-free planning, keep the menu simple...soup & sandwiches or maybe just chili. Play Christmas music and enjoy each other's company while you craft.*

Let's Have A Ball!

*Once you've chosen the projects for your crafting party, you may want to ask each guest to bring enough of a certain supply for everyone, such as glue, glitter or paint. Set up a separate workstation for each type of ornament with the supplies and how-to's right there...write the instructions clearly (remember, the larger the print, the easier it'll be to read!) and slide the paper into a sheet protector or laminate with clear self-adhesive vinyl.*

## PARTY INVITATION

Matching short ends, fold a 5½"x8" piece of green card stock in half for the card. Cut a dog-eared tag from white card stock to fit on the card, punch a hole in the ear end, then add a hole reinforcement. Tie gold metallic ribbon through the hole. Glue the tag to the card.

Cut a 1⅜" dia. circle from red paper; glue the circle to the tag for an ornament. Use a fine-point marker to draw a cap on the ornament…add some curly lines for a "hanger." Write your party particulars on the tag and additional information on the inside of the card.

Glue drops of gold glitter on the ornament and scatter hand-drawn snowflakes on the card for the finishing touches!

## EASY-TO-MAKE ORNAMENTS

Ornaments by the dozen in no time at all is what you'll have with these easy-to-do techniques!

### Beaded Ornaments

Use glue to draw designs or adhere designs or strips cut from scrapbook mounting adhesive sheets to pre-colored or frosted ornaments…when using glue, you'll want to do one design at a time. Cover the designs with micro beads. Hang glued ornaments to dry overnight.

### Etched Ornaments

Adhere designs cut from clear self-adhesive paper or stickers to clear glass ornaments. Paint the ornaments with 2 coats of frosted or colored spray finish. After the finish is dry, remove the shapes.

### Sticker Ornaments

Adhere pretty stickers to frosted ornaments, then add a tag to match.

*It's oh-so simple to dress up inexpensive glass ornaments with glittering micro beads, or you can create the look of etched glass using removable stickers and a spray-on frost finish. Complete instructions are on page 19.*

Here's another good party project: use metallic paint markers to hand-draw simple holiday designs (stars, snowflakes, trees or bows) on glass votive cups. You can even personalize them for great place markers on your dining table, or give them as little gifts!

Is the paint flaking off of your older glass ornaments? Buy glitter, faux jewels or sequins, or use beads from broken costume jewelry...glue them on to cover the old paint with sparkles.

# Country Snow Friends

*Kate, Holly & Mary Elizabeth can't resist the appeal of these country snowfolk! Craft a cute snow angel or a plaid-capped fellow from tea-dyed muslin, or paint a fanciful snowman on a rusted mitten-shaped tin ornament.*

## ANGEL ORNAMENT

Refer to *Tea Dyeing*, page 131, to dye a 6½"x8" piece of muslin. Allow the muslin to dry; press smooth and fold in half, matching short edges. Trace the pattern from page 135 onto tracing paper. Cut 2 angels from muslin. Leaving an opening for turning, sew the pieces together ¼" from the outer edges. Clip curves and turn the angel right-side out; stuff firmly with polyester fiberfill. Sew the opening closed.

Use cosmetic blush to color cheeks, then paint a brick-red nose on the angel. Sew 2 black beads to the angel for eyes; use a black fine-point permanent marker to draw eyebrows. Glue several strands of curly doll hair to the top of the angel, then glue a miniature faux garland around the head. Glue two 2½" rusted hearts to the back of the angel for wings. Stitch and knot a length of heavy thread at the top of the angel for a hanger.

## RUSTY TIN SNOWMAN ORNAMENT

Use a hammer and nail to punch a hole in a rusty mitten shape. Wipe the ornament with a tack cloth, then spray with matte sealer.

Paint 3 white circles for the snowman. Use your fingertip to lightly paint pink cheeks. Paint black eyes, an orange nose and 3 blue snowflake-shaped "buttons" on the snowman. Paint a green tree beside the snowman, then add a few "snowy" branches. *Spatter Paint*, page 131, the ornament, then apply a matte sealer. Add a wire hanger and you're done!

## STUFFED SNOWMAN

Refer to *Tea Dyeing*, page 131, to dye an 8"x17" piece of muslin. Allow the muslin to dry; press smooth. Trace the blue snowman pattern from page 138 onto tracing paper. Aligning the bottom of the pattern with the fold, pin the patterns to the muslin; cut out.

Leaving the top of the head open for turning, sew the sides together 1/4" from the edges. To make flat bottom, match each side seam to bottom fold line; sew across each corner 1 1/2" from point. Clip curves and turn the snowman right-side out. Fill the bottom 2" of the snowman with uncooked popcorn, then finish stuffing with polyester fiberfill. Sew the opening closed.

Paint a wooden star cut-out gold, then apply brown gel stain to the star; wipe away excess stain. Use cosmetic blush and a cotton swab to color cheeks, then paint an orange nose on the snowman. Use a black fine-point paint pen to add eyes and write a message on the star. Glue the star and 2 floss-tied buttons to the snowman.

Cut a 4"x5" hat and a 1"x12" scarf from homespun. Turning up a 3/4" wide cuff and overlapping ends at back, wrap the hat around the snowman's head and glue the overlapped edges together. Wrap and knot a piece of embroidery floss around the hat close to the snowman's head; knot the scarf around the neck.

Lightly *Spatter Paint*, page 131, the snowman with white paint.

# I Dig SNOW!

*Remember when you were a child and wished for snow with all your heart? Bring back that sense of anticipation and wonder with a whimsical sign!*

## "LET IT SNOW" SIGN

- tracing paper
- transfer paper
- 5"x12" wooden plaque
- blue and white acrylic paint
- paintbrushes
- four 2½" wooden snowflakes
- wood glue
- 2 thick wooden yardsticks
- two ¾" long wood screws
- black paint pen
- textured snow medium
- assorted white buttons
- craft staple gun
- rusted craft wire
- galvanized bucket
- gravel or sand
- polyester fiberfill

*Allow paint, paint pen and snow medium to dry after each application.*

**1.** Trace the "Let It Snow" pattern from page 135 onto tracing paper. Use transfer paper to transfer the words to the plaque. Paint the words blue and the wooden snowflakes white.

**2.** Glue the yardsticks together...make sure the numbers go the same direction. Glue the plaque to the yardstick (smaller numbers on the yardstick should be at the bottom). Working from the back, use screws to secure the plaque to the yardstick. Use the paint pen to write fun sayings along the yardstick.

**3.** Glue a button to the center of each snowflake. Glue three of the snowflakes to the yardstick and plaque. Use a craft stick to apply snow medium to the snowflakes, the top of the yardstick and along the top and side edges of the plaque...add a few dots of snow to the front of the plaque.

**4.** Stapling at the back as necessary and threading buttons onto the wire here and there, wrap wire loosely around the yardstick from bottom to top. At the top, wrap the wire around the remaining snowflake to create a "falling flake"; curl wire end. Wrap separate lengths of wire threaded with buttons around each snowflake; curl the wire ends.

**5.** Fill the bucket with gravel or sand; place the yardstick in the bucket. Layer lots of fiberfill "snow" in the top of the bucket.

*You can use the pattern for our stuffed snowman (shown on page 23) to draw a frosty friend on muslin…embellish him with buttons, homespun snippets and sponge-painted snowflakes.*

## SNOWMAN PORTRAIT

Apply primer, then 2 coats of blue paint to a wooden picture frame with an opening to fit an 8"x10" picture…you'll want your frame to be wide enough to stamp the snowflakes and words on it.

Cut a piece of cardboard to fit in the frame. Overlapping and gluing the edges to the back, cover the cardboard with muslin.

Use an iron-on transfer pen to trace the red snowman pattern, page 138, onto tracing paper. Place the fabric-covered cardboard in the frame and position the pattern, ink side down, on the muslin. Remove the frame, then iron to transfer the lines. Use a black permanent fine-point marker to draw over the lines. Paint the nose orange. Secure the cardboard in the frame.

For the hat, cut a 3" square of fabric. Fold the bottom edge up for a cuff, then fold the side edges to the wrong side until it's slightly wider than the head; spot glue the side edges at the cuff to secure. Knot thread around the top of the hat to gather it, then glue the hat to the snowman. For the scarf, cut two 1"x5" strips of fabric. For each strip, fold one end 1/4" to the wrong side, then glue the end at one side of neckline; knot the strips together and fray the ends. Glue 3 blue buttons down the front of the snowman. Add a little textured snow medium to the hat, scarf and buttons.

Using thinned white acrylic paint, randomly stamp snowflakes and a snowy message on the frame and muslin. Lightly *Spatter Paint*, page 131, the frame and portrait.

Paint a snowman face on a white lunch bag…just the right size for holding little surprises!

Turn a sideboard into a winter wonderland! Cover it with a white fleece blanket, then add reminders of winter fun…a pair of ice skates or snowshoes, a miniature sled and lots of pictures of the family building snowmen, skiing or bringing home the tree!

*"Frosty, in a coat of red,
With a scarf upon his head.
A ball of snow from head to toe,
Before the springtime he must go!"*

— Unknown

*"The more it snows, the more it goes on snowing. And nobody knows how cold my toes, how cold my toes are growing!"*

— A.A. Milne

*This darling chenille draft stopper is sure to bring a smile to your face! You'll want to keep him out all winter long.*

## SNOWMAN DRAFT STOPPER

- tracing paper
- white chenille fabric
- felt
- polar fleece
- homespun
- two ³/₄" dia. black buttons
- 5 orange buttons in graduated sizes
- embroidery floss
- hot glue gun
- assorted buttons for hat

*Match right sides and use a ¹/₄" seam allowance for all sewing unless otherwise indicated. Refer to Embroidery Stitches, page 132, and use 6 strands of floss for all embroidery.*

**1.** Enlarge the body pattern on page 136 by 125%; cut out. Trace the boot and arm patterns on page 137 onto tracing paper. Using patterns, cut 2 bodies and 4 arms from chenille and 4 boots from felt. Cut two 7"x13" legs from chenille, a 3"x33" scarf from homespun and a 2¹/₂"x6" tassel piece, a 14¹/₂" hat square and a 4"x14¹/₂" cuff from fleece.

**2.** Referring to the photo and working on right side of one body piece, sew black buttons to the face for eyes, work black cross stitches for the mouth, and sew 3 buttons down the front of the body. Stacking from largest to smallest, stack, then sew orange buttons to the face for the nose.

*(continued on page 121)*

Heap on more wood!
the wind is chill,
but let it whistle as
it will,
we'll keep our Christmas
merry still!
— SIR WALTER SCOTT —

# Jingle All the Way!

*Jingle your way to a jolly holiday! First, collect all the jingle bells you can find in all sizes, from jumbo to the very tiniest ones, then follow our super-simple how-to's to attach them to an evergreen wreath or a garland for your mailbox. Use your imagination to add merry music to table arrangements and your tree, too!*

## MAILBOX BELL SWAG

Make your home extra-special this year with a beautiful mailbox swag to match the wreath on your front door. Passersby will "ooh" & "aah" at the sparkly sight.

Wire a swag of artificial greenery securely to your mailbox...then, follow the same instructions for the wreath to attach bells to the swag.

Tie weatherproof wire-edged ribbon into a bow with 3 loops; wire the center of the bow to the swag.

It is by the benefit of Letters that absent friends are brought together.
-Seneca-

Hang jingle bells from ribbons, then tie on the doorknob for a welcoming jingle.

## JINGLE BELL WREATH

The old-fashioned sound of jingle bells puts everyone in the holiday spirit! Hang a jingle bell wreath on your door and every time you open it to welcome family & friends, they'll be greeted by the jolly jingle.

Begin with a plush artificial pine wreath...if it's not full enough, wire greenery picks in the bare spots to fill it out. Use floral wire to attach giant jingle bells here and there on the wreath. Next, wire three large bells together into a cluster; make several clusters, then wire each one to the wreath. Wire lots of assorted sizes of bells around the larger ones...try to cover the entire front of the wreath with bells. Hang your wreath from a heavy-duty wreath hanger.

# "Heart·Felt" Trims

*Country colors and the shapes of mittens, stars, hearts & hands make these festive felt trims the perfect decorations if you're country at heart. You can use our patterns, or pull out your holiday cookie cutters and create your own designs!*

### FELT ORNAMENTS

Mix & match bright colors of felt and some fun shapes to make whimsical ornaments.

Start by tracing the basic shape patterns from page 139 onto tracing paper. Using the patterns, different colors of felt and decorative-edge craft scissors for cutting some of the shapes, cut one shape the size of the pattern from felt, then larger and smaller sizes of the same shape from another color of felt. Layer and glue the shapes together.

If you are making mitten or hand ornaments, use the cuff pattern to cut a piece of felt the size of the pattern and a piece of chenille fabric just smaller than the pattern; glue the chenille to the felt, then glue the cuff to the hand or mitten. You may want to wrap decorative yarn around the cuff several times.

Sew on lots of tiny (and some not-so-tiny) jingle bells and loops of textured yarn...use the yarn to tie two mitten shapes together for a pair, or to string several ornaments together for a garland like the one on pages 32 and 33.

Trace your favorite cookie cutters onto colorful paper...hearts, stars, apples, gingerbread men; they'll make wonderful gift tags!

A good heart is worth gold. ~ SHAKESPEARE ~

*These cut-out decorations (instructions on page 30) are so versatile! Try stringing them together for a whimsical garland or mantel swag, or tie them on packages for "bonus" gifts. Another idea...stencil designs on a plain glass plate and fill with cookies for Santa! Turn to page 121 to decorate the plate, and the cookie recipe is on page 34.*

Kids big and little will love to make salt-dough ornaments using their favorite country-style cookie cutter shapes. Put a wooden matchstick in the soft dough before baking (break off the red tip first) for a hole you can string yarn or brown twine through. My daughter and I made several dozen of these ornaments when she was small and we were living on a sailboat. Now that she's grown and living in another part of the country, and about to start her own family, they are my most treasured ornaments, bringing back special memories every time I hang them on the tree.

— C.A. Long

It is great to have friends when one is young, but indeed it is still more so when you are getting old. When we are young, friends are, like everything else, a matter of course.

In the old days we know what it means to have them.

-Edvard Grieg-

# Gingerbread ✲ MAGIC

*It'll be hard to resist sampling these sweet gingerbread bowls and cookie ornaments, so be sure to make an extra batch for nibbling. Fill the bowls with greenery and cookie cut-outs for magical centerpieces, or pack with edible goodies to share with friends and neighbors.*

*"Had I but a penny in the world, thou shouldst have it for gingerbread."*

— William Shakespeare

## GINGERBREAD BOWL AND COOKIES

*This recipe works well for decorations, and it tastes good, too! Each fourth of the dough will make one bowl and several small cookies, or 9 heart-in-hand cookies.*

1 c. butter, softened
$^2/_3$ c. brown sugar, packed
$^1/_2$ c. sugar
$^2/_3$ c. dark corn syrup
$^1/_3$ c. molasses
4 eggs
$8^3/_4$ c. all-purpose flour
1 T. baking soda
1 t. salt
1 t. ground ginger
1 t. ground cloves
1 t. cinnamon
1 t. ground allspice
non-stick vegetable spray

Cream butter and sugars until fluffy. Beat in corn syrup, molasses and eggs until smooth. Combine flour, baking soda, salt and spices. Add dry ingredients to creamed mixture (mixture will be stiff). Divide dough into fourths. Wrap in plastic wrap and chill 2 hours. Coat the outside of a 1$^1/_2$-quart oven-proof glass bowl with cooking spray. On a sheet of plastic wrap sprinkled with flour, use a floured rolling pin to roll out one fourth of the dough into a $^1/_4$-inch-thick circle. Using plastic wrap, transfer dough to outside of bowl, pressing dough firmly onto bowl; remove plastic wrap. Trim excess dough from bottom edge of bowl. Place inverted bowl on an ungreased baking sheet. Use 1$^1/_4$-inch-wide heart-shaped or star-shaped cookie cutters to make cut-outs around bowl; set cut-out cookies aside. Bake bowl at 350 degrees for 22 to 28 minutes or until firm to the touch; allow to cool on bowl. Carefully remove gingerbread from bowl. Reroll excess dough and cut out additional heart and star cookies; place on a lightly greased baking sheet. Repeat with one fourth of dough for a second bowl. For heart-in-hand cookies, roll out one fourth of dough to $^1/_4$-inch thickness on a floured surface. Using a 4$^1/_2$"x 3$^3/_4$" cookie cutter, cut out cookies, leaving heart cut-out in place. Transfer cookies to a lightly greased baking sheet. Remove heart cut-outs and place on baking sheet with heart and star cut-outs. Bake larger cookies at 350 degrees for 8 to 10 minutes; bake smaller cookies 6 to 8 minutes. Transfer to a wire rack to cool. Makes 2 bowls and 18 heart-in-hand cookies.

*"Hot spice-gingerbread, hot! Hot! All hot! Come, buy my spice-gingerbread, smoking hot!"*

— 18th-century gingerbread vendors' cry

*Gingerbread* has been a favorite in Europe for centuries…in fact, gingerbread bakers even had their own guild, and there were laws against anyone else making the treat! If you'd lived during the Middle Ages, you might have purchased shaped gingerbread, impressed with a decorative religious design and dusted with powdered sugar, at the famous Christkindlmarkt, which is still held each December in Nuremberg, Germany. However, you'd hardly recognize it as the gingerbread we know and love today! The earliest recipes were made using a base of breadcrumbs with honey, a wide variety of spices and either ale, wine or brandy. In the 18th and 19th centuries, flour and molasses gradually replaced the breadcrumbs and honey, especially in America. The first gingerbread houses appeared during the Victorian era…they were probably inspired by German composer Englebert Humperdinck's opera, "Hänsel and Gretel."

# Holly Jolly Kitchen

*The Country Friends® added a few festive touches to their kitchens to put them in the holiday spirit! Holly painted an old soap dispenser and salt & pepper shakers, Mary Elizabeth stitched up homespun place mats and Kate made a beautiful etched plate and glass; etching instructions are on page 121.*

### SOAP BOTTLE AND SALT & PEPPER SHAKERS

Turn the vintage dispenser bottle you found at the flea market into a Christmas accent to hold your favorite dish soap. Before you start, refer to *Painting Techniques*, page 131, for some tips about painting from your Country Friends®.

Clean the bottle with alcohol and allow it to dry. Use paint pens or paint for glass to freehand a couple sprigs of pine, a few holly leaves and some red berries and the word "soap" on the bottle.

Since you already have the paint out, go ahead and paint the salt & pepper shakers you found, too! Just clean them like you did the soap bottle, then paint on a tree and some red dots...don't forget to label them!

## PLACEMAT & NAPKIN

A personalized placemat for each member of the family makes dinnertime even more special! These are easy to make...just remember to match right sides and use a ¹/₂" seam allowance for all sewing unless otherwise indicated.

For the placemat, cut one 11"x17" center and one 15"x21" backing from fabric. Cut two 3"x11" side strips, two 3"x21" top/bottom strips and two 6¹/₂" square pocket pieces from a coordinating fabric.

Sew the side strips, then the top and bottom strips to the center piece. Sew the pocket pieces together along 2 adjoining sides; turn right-side out.

Matching right sides and raw edges, place the pocket on the lower left corner of the center piece. Matching wrong sides and raw edges, pin the backing piece to the center piece. Leaving an opening for turning, sew the pieces together. Turn right-side out, sew opening closed and press.

Fold the corner of the pocket down, then sew a button to the flap to hold it in place.

For the napkin, cut a 17" square from fabric. Press each edge ¹/₄" to the wrong side; press ¹/₄" to the wrong side again and sew in place.

Thread a gold charm onto a length of ribbon, then use the ribbon to attach a handmade tag to the button on the placemat...refer to *Making a Tag or Label*, page 132, for how to's.

**E**very great man is always helped by everybody; for his gift is to get good out of all things and all persons.

~ JOHN RUSKIN.

## MOSAIC TRIVETS

There are never enough trivets around to set all the Christmas goodies on when the time comes! These not only serve that purpose, but they're quick & easy as well!

For each trivet base, you'll need either a small wooden-framed chalkboard or a wooden picture frame...if using a picture frame, you'll need to cut a piece of balsa wood to fit in the frame opening to raise the tiles slightly above the surface of the frame. Glue the wood in place.

Glue 1¹/₂" diameter wooden turnings to the bottom corners of the base for feet, then paint the base red and allow to dry. Spray the base with clear, thick, porcelain-finish glaze; allow to dry.

Apply masking tape around the opening in the base. Use tile adhesive to adhere ceramic tile squares or pieces of broken glass dishes in the base. Follow the manufacturer's instructions to apply tile grout around the pieces. Remove the tape and allow to dry.

*Decorate a tiny tree with cut-out cookies, tin cookie cutters and miniature kitchen gadgets.*

*Cranberry heart wreaths look so pretty hanging in your kitchen window. Simply push fresh cranberries tightly onto a length of wire that's been formed into a heart shape, then decorate with bows.*

*Christmas confetti plates add an elegant and very festive touch to any holiday occasion! Sprinkle any shape of holiday confetti…stars, snowflakes or Christmas trees…over a clear glass dinner plate. Place a second clear glass plate of the same size on top to secure the confetti and to place food on. You could also use fresh herb sprigs, old-fashioned paper snowflakes or children's art.*

*— Kim Smith*
*Brecksville, OH*

## DECORATED CANISTER SET

Embellished sheet magnets are a great way to liven up a set of metal canisters for Christmas…they're so easy, you may decide to make a set for each season!

For each canister, cut a piece of self-adhesive magnetic sheet to fit on the front of the canister; cut a piece of card stock the same size. Remove the paper from the magnet and adhere the card stock. Trimming to fit, glue a vintage postcard or tag to the card stock…make sure you leave room for the label.

Cut one strip each from decorative paper and clear vellum to fit on the remaining portion of the magnet. Use a craft glue stick to adhere the top edge of the vellum strip to the top of the paper strip. Working through the loop on a jingle bell, use 6 strands of embroidery floss to stitch through the top of the strips; glue the floss ends on the back to secure. Apply alphabet stickers to the vellum for labels or seasonal sayings, then glue the strip to the magnet.

# Santa's in Stitches!

*It's so much fun stitching this whimsical Santa, and what a terrific gift for special friends! We made a coordinating candle band using the pattern from Santa's hatband and trimmed more candles with ribbons, charms, stickers and more. The instructions for the stitched Santa and teddy are on page 121.*

A thought to ponder…Do you think Santa and Mrs. Claus leave their Christmas decorations up year 'round?

Santa's Wish List: wider (and cleaner!) chimneys, better hours, no pouting and…calorie-free cookies!

## CANDLE BANDS

### Heart Band

Using the pattern and key on page 142, Cross Stitch, page 131, a strip of hearts to fit around your candle on a 3" wide piece of 14 ct. Aida. Glue each long edge $\frac{1}{4}$" to the wrong side. Tear a 2" wide piece from red handmade paper the same length as the stitched piece; cut the strip in half lengthwise. Glue the paper strips to the stitched piece; add sticker borders along each edge. Overlapping and gluing ends at back, wrap band around candle.

### Charmed Band

Tear one wide and one narrow strip of coordinating colors of handmade paper to fit around the candle. Overlapping and gluing the ends at back, wrap the wide, then the narrow strip around the candle. For the tag, cut a dog ear tag from one color of paper. Embellish it with a square torn from the coordinating paper, a charm and sticker borders. Use a sheer ribbon to tie the tag to the candle.

### Noel Band

Tear a strip of handmade paper to fit around the candle. Leaving space for the "heart flowers," apply clear alphabet stickers to spell your favorite Christmas sentiment. Draw and color the "heart flowers" between the words. Overlapping and gluing the ends at back, wrap the band around the candle.

# Country Cottage Christmas

*Soft, country cottage colors bring a fresh look to traditional penny rug appliqués on our charming tree topper, skirt and ornaments. Use your imagination to mix-and-match colors to suit your own sense of style…you may want to try bright, bold primary hues, or even vivid jewel-tones!*

## PENNY RUG TREE

### Tree Topper

Trace the patterns, page 144, onto tracing paper. Cut two backgrounds from fabric and four leaves and one small circle from felt. Using pinking shears, cut one background and one large circle from felt. Layer and pin the pieces on a piece of felt to match the small circle...one fabric background piece will be left to cover the back of the topper. Using 3 strands of floss and referring to *Embroidery Stitches*, page 132, work *Running Stitches* along the edges of the pinked background and for veins on leaves. Work *Straight Stitch* "spokes" on small circle, then work *French Knots* through the holes of a button to attach it to the topper. Using 6 strands of floss, work *Blanket Stitches* along the edges of the fabric background. Trim the felt background piece with pinking shears. Glue the remaining fabric background over the back of the topper, then tack the center of a 12" length of ribbon to the back for a tie.

*(Ornaments and Tree Skirt continued on page 121)*

*Pull out your favorite Christmas collectibles to enhance your new holiday village…bottle brush trees, vintage figurines and ornaments are wonderful reminders of the past! To make the scalloped mantel scarf, turn to page 122.*

## CHRISTMAS VILLAGE

This village is so quiet and cozy you can imagine yourself walking through the freshly fallen snow to your quaint cottage.

For lighted houses, begin with a paper maché house with a removable roof. Cut a hole in the back to fit a clip-on light kit. Paint the house desired colors…paint the windowsills gold for extra shimmer from the light. Cover the windows on the inside of the house with vellum and the door with a piece of painted cardboard or craft foam to match the house.

Spruce up each house by adding shutters or door boards made from painted cardboard or craft foam; glue on a black bead for a doorknob and use a black permanent marker to draw "nail heads" on the boards. Apply textured snow medium to the roof and ground. Dust the snow with glitter flakes, then "plant" miniature bottle brush trees in the snow. Attach a colorfully beaded wire along the top of the house for Christmas lights…when you thread each bead onto the wire, give it a twist to secure it in place. For the

44

finishing touch, hang miniature wreaths on the doors and gables; secure the light kit in the back.

For the church or the barn, begin with a wooden birdhouse; paint the houses desired colors. Cut windows and doors from craft foam; paint the church windows to look like stained glass. Follow the instructions for the lighted houses to spruce up your church or barn.

Arrange the village on a mantel or table atop a layer of batting "snow"...you can cut small holes in the batting to run any cords through so they don't show.

*A holiday collection is like visiting old friends...and each time you add to the collection, you add a new memory.*

# Christmas Bouquets

*Even when it's cold and snowy outdoors, you can still enjoy beautiful fresh blossoms. Narcissus and amaryllis bulbs are plentiful this time of year, and easy to grow. Make use of your glassware collection for unique, interesting containers.*

## MILK GLASS PUNCH SET

### Candles

Turn vintage milk glass punch cups into festive candles. All you have to do is purchase waxed wicks and creamy wax in your favorite holiday scent and color, then follow the manufacturer's instructions to add the wick and wax to the cups. Simple, beautiful and quick!

### Planter

Amaryllis are wonderful Christmas flowers! You can showcase your natural or artificial blooms in a milk glass punch bowl. For natural flowers, simply plant your bulb in the punch bowl in early November to flower by Christmas. For artificial flowers, fill the bowl with floral foam…"plant" the stems in the foam. Lace ribbon around the stalks, then cover the foam with Spanish moss.

Be careful going in search of Adventure— it's ridiculously easy to find. -WILLIAM LEAST HEAT MOON-

*Vivid poinsettias add a splash of color anywhere! A creamy milk glass vase contrasts beautifully with the deep crimson leaves.*

Have you ever heard the legend of the Christmas poinsettia? Years ago, in many Mexican villages it was the custom for each person to place a gift for baby Jesus on the church altar on Christmas Eve. It's said that an angel appeared to a poor child, who was crying because he had nothing to give, and told him to pluck some weeds from the side of the path. When the boy placed the weeds on the altar, they were magically transformed into beautiful crimson poinsettias. Ever since, the poinsettia has been called "The Flower of the Holy Night" in Mexico.

## JADITE CANISTERS AND BUTTER DISH

Looking for something new to decorate with for Christmas? Try something old! A collection of jadite canisters and a covered butter dish make unique containers. Simply arrange your cut flowers in the canisters, then use the lids as drip trays for candles tied with sheer ribbon…plant crocus in the lid of the butter dish in time for Christmas blooms.

make time for

a little holiday relaxation

This is a Yugoslavian tradition that we learned while we were in Seattle. On St. Nicholas Day, December 6th, place one-fourth cup of whole wheat berries in a shallow dish and sprinkle with water. Each day afterward, sprinkle lightly with water to encourage germination...a spray bottle is perfect for this. Let the sprouts continue to grow until Christmas Eve, when they should reach their full height of 6 inches. Place a pillar or votive candle in the center and light. The new growth of wheat symbolizes prosperity, health and happiness in the coming year. You can even deliver a bag of wheat berries tied with a red ribbon along with the traditional story and directions to friends just before St. Nicholas Day.

— Pat Fessel
Haines, OR

Fill a galvanized bucket with pebbles. Tuck in a variety of flowering bulbs...tulips, daffodils or hyacinths are all pretty! Add water around the pebbles, just barely covering them, and tie on a raffia bow. In just a few weeks, you'll have a springtime bouquet.

Arrange white poinsettias in cobalt-blue vases and pitchers...line them up on your mantel and twine with evergreen boughs and tiny white lights...beautiful!

There's no place like home at Christmas time.

# Kid Friendly

*Christmas is custom-made for kids! Why not let them help get ready for the big day? Youngsters will love crafting gifts like personalized bookmarks, a cookie jar for Dad or making plaster handprints that you can frame for grandparents (see page 122 for the framed handprint instructions). To please a little baker, turn the page to decorate an apron, then fill the pockets with real cooking utensils.*

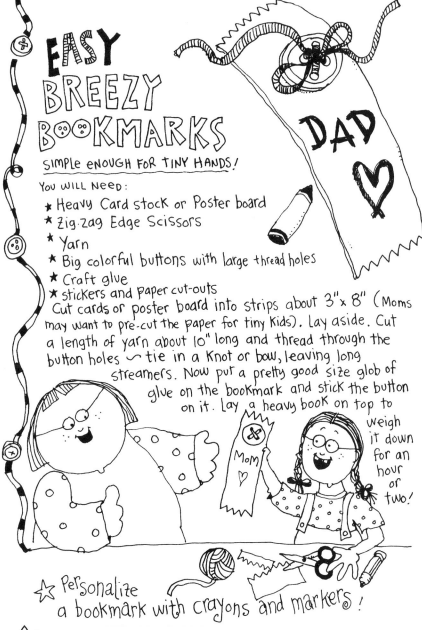

## EASY BREEZY BOOKMARKS

### SIMPLE ENOUGH FOR TINY HANDS!

YOU WILL NEED:

★ Heavy Card stock or Poster board
★ Zig-zag Edge Scissors
★ Yarn
★ Big colorful buttons with large thread holes
★ Craft glue
★ stickers and paper cut-outs

Cut cards or poster board into strips about 3" x 8" (Moms may want to pre-cut the paper for tiny kids). Lay aside. Cut a length of yarn about 10" long and thread through the button holes ～ tie in a Knot or bow, leaving long streamers. Now put a pretty good size glob of glue on the bookmark and stick the button on it. Lay a heavy book on top to weigh it down for an hour or two!

☆ Personalize a bookmark with crayons and markers!

DAD ♡

Use Your Imagination.

RUDOLPH

BLUE

*Brush your little one's hand with red or green acrylic paint, then press it onto a square of unbleached muslin; let dry. Use the fabric to make a stocking or pillow for Grandma!*

Natalie
4-2-02

## GOLF JAR

Send Dad to his favorite golf course with a jar of cookies to munch on along the way!

Following the manufacturer's instructions to knead and dry, spread a smooth layer of green modeling compound over the top and sides of a clean jar lid. Roll some white modeling compound into a ball shape to fit the lid; use the end of a paintbrush to push "golf ball dimples" into the ball. Press the ball into the compound on the lid, then allow it all to dry. Fill the jar with cookies and replace the lid. Tie a length of ribbon around the neck of the jar, then attach a tag you made by referring to *Making a Tag or Label* on page 132.

DAD
From Kyle

The scenes of Childhood are the memories of future years.

—Jo. Choules

## CHILD'S APRON

Let a youngster help make new Christmas memories and still keep their clothes clean with this easy, festive apron embellished with a "loving" heart.

Start by turning the bottom of a canvas apron up 6½" for the pocket; sew the pocket in place along the existing side stitching.

Use a standard-size grommet tool to attach grommets at 1" intervals, ½" from the side edges of the apron; attach 5 grommets at 1" intervals down the center of the pocket. Beginning at the lower right corner, lace ⅜" wide red ribbon around apron edge through grommets; glue ribbon across front top edge of apron, then lace down opposite side. Glue ribbon ends to back of apron to secure. Gluing ends to back of apron to secure, thread ribbon through the grommets at the center of the pocket. Tie a ribbon bow; safety pin it to the top center of the pocket.

Follow manufacturer's instructions to adhere fusible red felt letters spelling the child's name across the top of the apron. For the patch, cut a 5¾" square from fabric and fusible interfacing. Place the fusible side of the interfacing on the right side of the fabric; using a ¼" seam allowance and leaving a small opening for turning, sew all edges together. Turn the patch right-side out and fuse to apron just below the name. Trace the heart pattern from page 142 onto fusible interfacing…finish the heart just like you did the patch, then fuse it to the center of the patch. Referring to *Embroidery Stitches*, page 132, work *Running Stitches* along the edges of the heart and a *Cross Stitch* at each corner of the patch. Notch the ends of a 3" length of ⅝" wide green ribbon. Fold the ribbon in half and tack the fold to the heart; sew several red buttons over the fold.

*It's easy to assemble a cookie-decorating kit with a personalized apron…throw in Christmasy cookie cutters, tubes of colored icing, decorating sugar crystals, and other cookie-making essentials. Your pint-size chef will have a ball!*

Kids can make clever chalkboard gift bags for their teachers' presents in no time…simply use white paint pens to write greetings and draw designs on black gift bags. Tuck the gifts inside, fold the top over and punch two holes in the middle, then slip a pencil through the holes to secure the top of the bag.

After hours of Christmas cookie baking, it's a nice touch for a child to be able to go to the freezer and pull out a moistened, folded face cloth that's been soaked in fresh lemon water. It's most refreshing to their floury little faces and hands.

— Jan Kouzes

Decorating sugar cookies is a family tradition. We set aside one night when everyone, even visitors, joins in. We mainly do gingerbread men, creating everything from football players to self portraits, all with frosting and lots of imagination.

— Sally Burke
Lansing, MI

"Everyone can know the special magic of waiting for St. Nick on Christmas Eve. Everyone can be a child at Christmas; all we have to do is just believe."

— Unknown

# Wrap Up the Holidays

Handmade gifts are the best way we know to share warm holiday hugs with special people! This year, surprise friends & family with warm and cozy granny-square hat and scarf sets, or share decorative touches like throw pillows. Don't forget the family pets...how about a painted peg rack to hold Spotty's leash and collar? Of course, you'll need creative packaging, tags and cards. We've got lots of great ideas to help you wrap up the season in style!

*You won't believe how simple it is to add creative touches to all your holiday gifts! Tips for making customized tags are on page 56; turn to page 123 to find festive gift wrap ideas.*

## TAG IDEAS

Let the kids of all ages play...imagine the fun!

Decorate a tiny flat brown paper bag to put the nametag in, or start with a base tag cut from card stock or decorative paper. Add a background cut from decorative paper if you'd like...use decorative-edge craft scissors to do some of the trimming. Use rubber stamps or stickers to embellish the tags (Kate spent 3 days checking out all the new scrapbooking stickers and decorations at a craft store!), then write the name on with paint pens, stickers, glitter gel pens or whatever you have on hand. Glue miniature greenery or charms on the tag to add dimension. Finish off by punching a hole in the tag, then thread with a ribbon, raffia or small cord hanger.

Instead of using wrapping paper, make drawstring bags in different sizes and fabrics. They can be used year after year to "wrap" your gifts.

— Margaret Clark

Color photocopies of family photographs and snapshots are perfect for making heart-felt greeting cards. Cut the copies using decorative-edge scissors, then use spray adhesive to apply to the front of a plain note card and write your holiday messages inside!

*Fun ways to make holiday memories…give a set of festively trimmed note cards and envelopes or a scrapbook featuring a hand-colored St. Nick (instructions for the Santa memory album are on page 123). Transform colorful card stock shapes into "fun-tastic" gift tags with silvery embroidery floss and mini ornaments.*

## CHRISTMAS STATIONERY

Make this fun stationery to write your after-Christmas thank-you notes on…or to give several as a gift themselves!

Start with blank note cards and matching envelopes. If you desire, trim decorative paper to cover the front of the card, then glue it on. Adhere stickers to the fronts of the cards…we used border stickers, glitter-adorned trees, stocking and wreath stickers, frame and snowman stickers and greeting stickers. If you can't find a sticker the shape you want, cut the

shapes out of decorative paper and use a craft glue stick to attach it to the card.

You can also use decorative-edge craft scissors to trim the card fronts along the border sticker…apply stickers to the exposed area of the inside of the card. Stamp greetings on the cards.

For a matching envelope, line the inside of the envelope, under the gummed edge, with coordinating paper, then add stickers to the outside of the envelope.

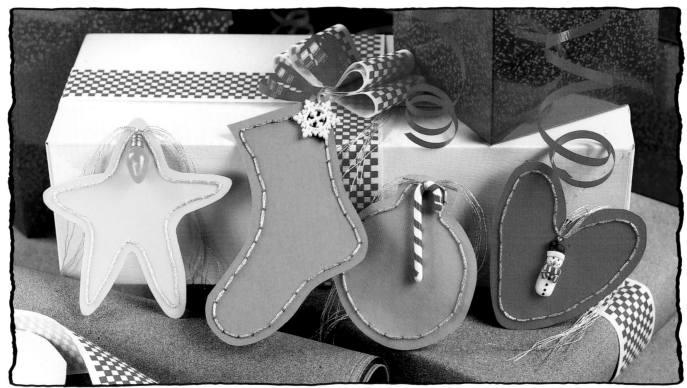

## SEWN GIFT TAGS

Trace the patterns, page 143, or draw around big cookie cutters, onto tracing paper. Use the patterns to cut tags from Christmasy colors of card stock. Leaving long streamers of metallic floss and using coordinating floss to match the cut-out, tack the metallic floss along the edges of the tag. Attach a charm to the streamers and tack in place. Use the streamers to tie your one-of-a-kind tag to your package.

*Make personalized gift wrap out of your family photos! Take your snapshots to your local printer and have them copied onto large sheets of paper. Use red raffia as your "ribbon." It's great for small packages! Copy the kids' artwork to wrap gifts for Grandma…she'll love it!*

*Hang the Christmas cards you receive on lengths of jute or evergreen garland; hang them around doorways or windows. Save the cards for next year; you can cut out the motifs to make wonderful gift tags.*

# Pretty Pillows to Give

Who can resist snuggling up with a pile of pretty pillows? Not the Country Friends®! Mary Elizabeth salvaged her mom's favorite apron and used it to "dress" a chenille pillow, and Kate transformed an old embroidered pillowcase into a country cushion. Holly chose vintage hankies and crocheted pot holders to embellish her pillows. Turn to page 123 to learn how!

Are you looking for inventive ways to use those vintage pillowcases, lovely embroidered towels and other fabric treasures you've collected at flea markets and yard sales? Turn 'em into darling decorative details to share (or keep for yourself!). Fold a tea towel or pillowcase over a curtain rod for an instant valance, or use old embroidered linens to make sweet pillows. If the item is damaged, cut out the pretty parts and appliqué them onto bed or table linens, towels, curtains...use your imagination to create one-of-a-kind accessories!

Oversize fabric napkins in colorful prints make terrific pillows! Just place two napkins with wrong sides facing, stitch three sides together, slip in a pillow form or fill with batting, then slipstitch the last side closed.

60

# Crocheted Cozies

*Keep youngsters warm & toasty with these crocheted cozies! The rough-and-tumble look of the striped cap and scarf is just right for a little boy…and it's a great way to make use of your yarn scraps. Little girls will love the delicate snowflake set, and extra-soft yarn makes it especially cozy. For complete instructions for making each set in small, medium or large youth sizes, see page 124.*

For complete instructions for making each set in small, medium or large youth sizes, see page 124.

Lead the life that
and friendly to
and you will be
HAPPY

– CHA

# for Kids

make you kindly
one around you,
prised what a
fe you will live.

SCHWAB-

Give your favorite youngster a new lunch box with his special heroes on it. Fill it with Christmas cookies!

Make a festive drum…just wrap an empty coffee can or oatmeal container with bright paper and attach gold cord. So fun for a gift package!

Little girls love to dress up dolls. Along with that new doll, give her colorful rolls of fabric remnants, safety scissors and bits of ribbons and lace for making doll fashions. The best part of the gift…spend an afternoon helping her invent new styles.

# Nifty Notions

*Everyone loves handcrafted gifts, but it's so hard to find time to make them. We've got great ideas that you can finish in no time, and they're easy on your budget, too! Embellish a ready-to-wear sweater with a frosty friend, or create a nostalgic memo board using flea market finds. For more nifty notions, just turn the page.*

### APPLIQUÉD SNOWMAN SWEATER

Any little girl will have frosty fun when she wears this whimsical snowman on her sweater.

Trace the patterns from page 149 onto tracing paper. Using the patterns, cut one hat and one scarf from fabric (Kate used pieces from her Grandma's old quilt top!) and one snowman from plush felt; cut 2 noses from orange felt.

Stack the nose pieces, sew the sides together, then sew the wide end of the nose to the snowman's face. Use embroidery floss to attach small black snaps to the face for eyes and large black snaps to the body for buttons.

Pin the snowman on a sweater; use embroidery floss to work *Straight Stitches*, page 132, along the snowman edges. Pin the hat on the snowman, then work *Blanket Stitches*, page 132, along the edges…work *Blanket Stitches* along the scarf edges. Arrange the scarf on the snowman and tack in place.

## QUILTED MESSAGE BOARD

Cut a piece of foam core board to fit in a wooden picture frame. Wrapping the edges to the back and hot gluing to secure, cover the foam core with a piece cut from an old quilt. Arrange lengths of ribbon across the covered foam core to form evenly spaced diamonds…glue the ends of the ribbon to the back of the board.

Use wire to attach a button at each ribbon crisscross…you may need to use a nail to poke holes through the board. Twist wire ends together at the back of the board and trim ends as needed.

Secure the message board in the frame, then attach picture hangers to the back of the frame.

Use household adhesive to glue colorful buttons to the tops of pushpins for decorative tacks.

*You can often find quilt tops that were never sewn together for a great price at flea markets, antique shops or tag sales. Stitch them into Teddy bears or pillows for heartwarming gifts.*

*Fragrant votive candles in decorated holders are great, quick little gifts…and they're inexpensive, too! Cut cinnamon sticks the same height as a glass votive; glue them around the holder and tie with a strip of homespun for a country look. Shiny, flexible gold, silver or copper wire is easy to find at craft and hardware stores; wrap it around glass votives for holiday sparkle.*

*More quick creations: Add elegant touches to the cover of a store-bought journal to give to a friend…decorate one for yourself, too! Girls of all ages will appreciate "charming" bracelets crafted with colorful beads. For a travelin' man (or woman!), how about a set of laminated luggage tags? Instructions for the luggage tags are on page 128.*

## RIBBON AND BUTTON JOURNAL

Help a friend start recording her favorite holiday memories with words and pictures in this decorated journal. We used a 10" square, spiral-bound journal and the instructions given fit this size…if using a smaller journal, adjust the center design to fit.

Tear a 9" square from handmade paper; cut an 8" square from card stock, then cut a 7¹/₂" square from corrugated card stock. Center, layer and glue the pieces on the journal.

For the center design, cut a 3¹/₂"x4¹/₂" piece of decorative paper and a 3"x4" piece of muslin. Cut a triangle-shaped tree from green ribbon to fit on the muslin piece; use a craft glue stick to adhere the tree to the muslin. Using one strand of silver metallic embroidery floss and "stringing" it across the tree, tack silver seed beads along the sides of the tree. Color a brown trunk on the tree. Use the craft glue stick to adhere the center of the muslin piece to the decorative paper piece; use a sewing machine to zig-zag stitch along the muslin edges.

Cut a label from card stock; use stickers to personalize it. Arrange the center design, label and 3 buttons on the journal; glue in place. Cut a 15" length of ribbon. Thread a shank button onto the center of the ribbon; hot glue the button to the top center of the decorative paper. Spot glue the ribbon along the top and side edges of the paper, folding the ribbon at the corners. Threading from opposite directions, thread the ends of the ribbon through another shank button; hot glue the button to the bottom center of the paper. Trim the ribbon ends.

**Nothing** makes a woman more beautiful than the belief that she is **beautiful**.
— SOPHIA LOREN

## CHARMED BRACELET

Thread Christmasy colors of assorted beads with seasonal charms or buttons here & there onto stretchy jewelry cord to fit around your wrist. Without stretching the cord, knot the ends together close to the beads, then trim the ends. Dab a dot of clear glue on the knot to keep it secure. In no time at all, you have a one-of-a-kind bracelet.

Make an easy Christmas pomander: Simply use a toothpick to make holes in an orange and insert whole cloves into the openings, then roll orange in a mixture of equal parts orrisroot powder and cinnamon; let it "cure" for about four weeks. Add a ribbon for hanging…so fragrant!

Deliver a small potted and decorated Christmas tree to a friend who can replant it outdoors in the spring. As the tree grows, it will be a constant reminder of your friendship!

Buy rolls and rolls of beautifully patterned ribbons throughout the year when they're on sale. Tartan plaids, festive French-wired designs and shimmering metallics will dress your packages handsomely throughout the year, and especially at Christmas!

Throughout the year I purchase small, inexpensive items such as key chains, costume jewelry, little toys or cassette tapes. Before Christmas, I wrap and tag the boxes and arrange them on a decorated tray. After Christmas dinner, while family and guests linger over dessert and coffee, I sneak upstairs to get the tray of "dessert gifts." It's a nice surprise at the end of the day and helps make the Christmas magic last a little longer.

— Anne Farnese

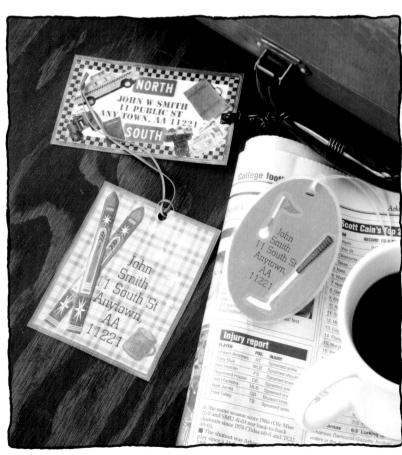

Oh Christmas Tree!

## BUTTON TREE PIN

What a festive and oh-so-simple pin to make!

Paint a small tree-shaped wooden cut-out green with a brown trunk (we used a 3" tall cut-out); allow the paint to dry. Glue layers of assorted green buttons to the tree…scatter a few tiny gold metal stars and some red baby buttons on the tree and glue in place. Glue a pin clasp to the back of the tree.

For the card, stamp a message at the bottom of a 4¼"x6" piece of card stock. Layer and glue pieces of decorative paper on the card. Cut a slit at the center of the card to accommodate the pin clasp, then press the clasp through the slit.

## "SEASON'S GREETINGS" WALL HANGING

- tan, brown, white, gold and 2 shades of green and red felt
- blue/black and red/black checked flannel
- paper-backed fusible web
- tan, black, dark or brick red and white embroidery floss
- tissue paper
- fabric glue
- jute

*Refer to Embroidery Stitches, page 132, before beginning project. Use 6 strands of black embroidery floss for all stitching unless otherwise indicated.*

1. Cut one 13½"x21" background from tan felt and one 10½"x18" sky from blue flannel. Cut four 1¾" corner squares from brown felt. Tear three 1"x5" hanging strips from red flannel.

2. Use the patterns from pages 150 to 152 and follow *Making Appliqués, page 130,* to make the following appliqués: house from red flannel; chimney top and door from tan felt; ground snow, roof snow and smoke swirls from white felt; moon, one of each star and 2 windows from gold felt; tree trunk, roof and chimney from brown felt; tree and 14 leaves from green felt; and 24 berries from red felt.

3. Pin one brown square to each corner of the tan background piece; work tan *Blanket Stitches* along the edges of each square and black *Blanket Stitches* along the edges of the background piece. Press the sky edges ¼" to the wrong side; center and pin to the tan background piece. Pin the ground snow at the bottom of the sky, then work *Blanket Stitches* along all the snow edges; work *Running Stitches* along the remaining sky edges.

4. Set the roof snow and smoke appliqués aside. Overlapping as necessary, arrange and fuse the remaining appliqués on the wall hanging. Work *Running Stitches* along house, chimney top, tree trunk, moon and stars edges; *Blanket Stitches* along the tree, chimney, door and roof edges; and red *Cross Stitches* on the tree.

(continued on page 128)

The joy that comes in giving Christmas gifts is not the hasty word of thanks, the gift given in return or even the happy laughter of little children but the pleasure of giving to old and young, to rich and poor, the wide world over. Oh, how I should like to be Santa Claus on Christmas Day!

EDWIN GROVER

Every pet owner knows that "pets are people, too!" Be sure to include your animal friends in the festivities. How about a colorful peg rack to organize Rover's leashes and collars or a personalized placemat for Muffin? Spotty says to throw in some tasty snacks and chew toys, too!

I have enjoyed the happiness of the world; I have loved.
-R. SCHILLER-

## LEASH RACK

*Refer to Painting Techniques, page 131, for some helpful tips on painting from your Country Friends®. Allow primer, paint and sealer to dry after each application.*

Remove the pegs from a wooden peg rack; apply primer to the rack and pegs. Paint a black & white checkerboard stripe around the edges of the rack; paint the front yellow. Paint the pegs and a ¼" wide stripe along the front edges of the rack light blue.

Refer to Lettering, page 132 to add names to the rack...paint the letters red and outline them with a black permanent marker. Paint any "O's" to look like a ball, then add marker "bounce lines" across the rack. Paint black paw prints on the rack.

Very lightly sand the rack and pegs for an aged look; wipe with a tack cloth. Glue the pegs in the rack. Apply 2 to 3 coats of matte clear acrylic sealer to the rack.

## PET PLACEMAT

Your cat will feel it has truly won your heart when you make it its very own personalized placemat to dine on.

Enlarge the pattern on page 153 by 136%.

Apply 2 coats of white gesso, then the desired basecoat color, to the wrong side of an 11"x14" piece of vinyl. Use transfer paper to transfer the pattern to the center of the vinyl.

Paint the design...use a black permanent marker to outline the designs and add details and to draw a dashed line around the inside of the border. Personalize the placemat by adding your cat's name (you can refer to *Lettering*, page 132, for some easy ways to do lettering). Finish off with 2 to 3 coats of clear acrylic sealer.

# GOODIES FOR GIVING

Looking for some great gift ideas? Step into the kitchen with Kate, Holly & Mary Elizabeth! They're cooking up all sorts of goodies for giving, from creative cookies to savory snacks and merry mixes…and of course, Kate insisted on including some heavenly treats for her fellow chocoholics. You'll also find fun packaging ideas, like festively trimmed mittens, painted plates, fancy decorated bags and lots more. Put on your apron and come on in!

*Many of our recipes, including these yummy Fruitcake Cookies (see page 79), make enough to share with lots of friends. Just bag 'em up and pass 'em out!*

# Tantalizing T·R·E·A·T·S

*Whether you need a bunch of little gifts or one extra-special surprise, take a look at these tempting treats…you're sure to find just the right recipe!*

*For a refreshing change of pace, pack a jar of sassy Shrimp Salsa and some crispy tortilla chips in a beaded cardboard bag (instructions on page 128).*

## SHRIMP SALSA
*This is a great hit whenever we serve it.*

2¹/₂ lbs. cooked shrimp, peeled and
    chopped
24-oz. jar mild salsa
2 c. fresh cilantro, chopped
2 c. tomatoes, chopped
¹/₂ c. red onion, chopped
2 T. lime juice
tortilla chips

Combine all ingredients in a large bowl. Cover and chill 8 hours or overnight. Serve with tortilla chips.
        Kathy Staley
        Boyd, TX

## HOLIDAY CHEESE BALL
*This tasty recipe is one we always enjoy on Christmas Day!*

1 t. onion juice
1 t. Worcestershire sauce
¹/₂ c. fresh parsley, chopped
8-oz. pkg. cream cheese
¹/₂ lb. shredded sharp Cheddar
    cheese
4-oz. wedge blue cheese
³/₄ c. chopped pecans, divided
Garnish: pecans and fresh parsley

Combine first 6 ingredients together in a mixing bowl; stir in ¹/₂ cup pecans and shape into a ball. Roll cheese ball in remaining ¹/₄ cup of pecans. Garnish with whole pecans and fresh parsley. Let stand at room temperature one hour before serving.
        Mary Kay Drayton
        Fenton, MI

## CANDY BAR CAKE
*Warning! Extremely rich!*

4  2.13-oz. chocolate-covered
   nougat candy bars*
1 c. butter, divided
2 c. sugar
4 eggs
$1/2$ t. baking soda
$1^1/4$ c. buttermilk
$2^1/2$ c. all-purpose flour
1 c. chopped pecans

Stirring frequently, melt candy bars and $1/2$ cup butter in a saucepan over low heat. Cream sugar and $1/2$ cup butter; beat in eggs. Gradually, beat in candy mixture. Stir baking soda into buttermilk. Alternately add flour and buttermilk; blend well. Stir in pecans. Bake in a greased Bundt® pan at 325 degrees for one hour and 10 minutes. Ice when cool.

Icing:
$2^1/2$ c. sugar
1 c. evaporated milk
6-oz. pkg. semi-sweet chocolate
   chips
1 c. marshmallow creme
$1/2$ c. butter

Combine sugar and milk; cook over medium heat stirring constantly until mixture reaches the soft ball stage, or 234 to 240 degrees on a candy thermometer. Add chocolate chips, marshmallow creme and butter. Stir until smooth; pour over cake.
**\*Note:** We used 3 Musketeers® candy bars for this cake.

*Charlotte Wolfe*
*Ft. Lauderdale, FL*

*Share platefuls of fun with your favorite chocoholics with French Chocolate Balls or a scrumptious Candy Bar Cake. Follow the easy instructions on page 128 to decoupage clear plates.*

## FRENCH CHOCOLATE BALLS
*So rich, so chocolatey, crunchy on the outside and soft on the inside...a chocolate-lover's dream!*

2 eggs
$2/3$ c. sugar
1 t. vanilla extract
$2^1/3$ c. almonds, finely ground
$1/3$ c. all-purpose flour
4 oz. unsweetened chocolate,
   grated
$1/2$ t. cinnamon
powdered sugar, sifted

Beat eggs, sugar and vanilla until light and fluffy. Add remaining ingredients and beat well. Pat dough into a ball and chill one hour. Shape dough into small, one-inch diameter balls. Roll each ball in powdered sugar and place on a baking sheet lined with parchment paper. Allow to dry for 4 hours in refrigerator on baking sheet. Bake at 475 degrees for 3 minutes, or until they've formed a light crust. Allow to cool 10 minutes on baking sheet; transfer to cooling rack. Makes about 4 dozen.

## MERRY BERRY SYRUP

*Drizzle your pancakes or waffles with this tasty syrup!*

1²/₃ c. water
²/₃ c. sugar
2 T. corn syrup
2 T. cornstarch
3-oz. pkg. raspberry gelatin mix
8-oz. pkg. frozen raspberries, thawed
8-oz. pkg. frozen blueberries, thawed

Stir together water, sugar, corn syrup and cornstarch; pour into a 2-quart saucepan. Cook over medium heat, stirring constantly, until mixture thickens. Remove saucepan from heat and stir in gelatin until dissolved. Fold in raspberries and blueberries; gently stir. Serve over pancakes or waffles. Makes 8 servings.

*Jill Valentine*
*Jackson, TN*

## COMET'S WHITE CHOCOLATE CRUNCH

*A favorite of children and reindeer everywhere!*

10-oz. pkg. mini pretzels
5 c. doughnut-shaped oat cereal
5 c. bite-size crispy corn cereal squares
2 c. peanuts
16-oz. pkg. candy-coated chocolates
2 12-oz. pkgs. white chocolate chips
3 T. oil

Combine first 5 ingredients in a very large bowl; set aside. Melt chocolate chips with oil in a double boiler; stir until smooth. Pour over cereal mixture; mix well. Spread mixture equally onto 3 wax paper-lined baking sheets; allow to cool. Break into bite-size pieces; store in airtight containers. Makes 5 quarts.

*Donna Nowicki*
*Center City, MN*

## Barbecue Pecans
*a recipe from Karen Moran ★ Navasota, TX*

4 c. pecans
½ c. butter
2 t. seasoned salt
1 t. barbecue sauce
½ t. hot pepper sauce
1 t. liquid smoke
2 T. Worcestershire sauce

Mix all ingredients together; spread in a 13"x9" baking sheet. Bake at 300 degrees for 25 to 30 minutes. Stir every 8 to 10 minutes. Makes one quart.

★ **IDEA!** Pack a small plastic bag full of treats and pop it inside a mitten or glove for a holiday give-away gift. Shop after-season for on-sale mittens for next year!

## BROWN SUGAR MUSTARD

*Its brown sugar taste is great with Italian sausage or bratwurst!*

½ c. dry mustard
½ c. cider vinegar
2 eggs
¼ c. brown sugar, packed
⅛ c. oil
½ t. Worcestershire sauce

Blend mustard and vinegar together in a double boiler; add eggs and whisk until smooth. Stir in remaining ingredients; simmer 5 minutes. Cool and pour into a covered jar. Keep refrigerated. Makes one cup.

*Dana Cunningham*
*Lafayette, LA*

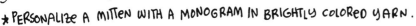

★ PERSONALIZE A MITTEN WITH A MONOGRAM IN BRIGHTLY COLORED YARN.

## EARL'S CARAMEL CORN

*Remember to share with neighbors and friends...that's what makes this candy the sweetest.*

12 qts. popped popcorn
2 c. flaked coconut
2 1/2 c. water
3 c. sugar
2 c. brown sugar, packed
1 1/4 c. corn syrup
2 t. salt
4 c. Spanish peanuts
2 t. vanilla extract
1/2 c. butter
1/4 t. baking soda

Toss popcorn and coconut; place in a large roasting pan and set aside in a 250-degree oven to warm. Heat water, sugars and syrup in a heavy saucepan to soft-ball stage, or 234 to 240 degrees on a candy thermometer. Add salt and peanuts; heat to soft-crack stage, or 270 to 290 degrees on a candy thermometer. Remove from heat; add vanilla and butter, stirring until melted. Add baking soda; stir until creamy. Pour over warm popcorn mixture; toss until well coated. Spread on greased baking sheets to cool. Makes 12 quarts.

Shawna Searle
Burley, ID

Treat a coffee or cocoa lover to a festive mug filled with chocolate spoons and cinnamon sticks for stirring...include some crunchy biscotti for dunking.

## CHOCOLATE STIRRING SPOONS

*An easy gift to make for the coffee lovers on your list.*

12-oz. pkg. semi-sweet chocolate
  chips
2 t. shortening
35 to 45 heavy plastic spoons

Line baking sheets with parchment paper. Place chocolate chips in a microwave-safe bowl; microwave on medium power for 2 minutes or until melted, stirring every 30 seconds. To thin chocolate, add shortening to chocolate; gently stir. Dip each plastic spoon in chocolate mixture to cover the bowl of the spoon; place on parchment paper for chocolate to set. Cool thoroughly before wrapping. Makes 35 to 45 spoons.

*Embellished mittens make cozy containers for merry munchies, like Comet's White Chocolate Crunch and Barbecue Pecans, or a jar of Brown Sugar Mustard. The packaging tips are on page 128.*

*Deliver stacks of Buttery Cinnamon Stars in clear tumblers with instructions to "just add milk" (see below). You could even apply the stickers directly to the glasses for creative holiday keepsakes!*

## AND Speaking of COOKIES...

↪Here's a great way to package cookies for gift-giving ⌣ easy, elegant & keeps the cookies from crumbling!

Find some clear glasses that are fairly tall, like so: (you know, the kind you sip those good, fruity, frosty drinks out of)...
now,
bake round cookies just a bit smaller than the glass in circumference... drop the cookies in carefully, stacking them inside the glass on top of each other 'til the glass is full.
Finish it off with a wired ribbon tied around the glass vertically. →
Add a sticker on the glass, over the ribbon, for a last touch...
*you're ready to deliver!*

JUST ADD MILK

## BUTTERY CINNAMON STARS

*Festive little butter-rum cookies.*

1 c. unsalted butter, softened
1 c. sugar
2¹/₄ c. almonds, finely ground
1 egg
2¹/₂ t. cinnamon
zest of one orange
¹/₄ c. dark rum or orange juice
3¹/₃ c. all-purpose flour
¹/₂ t. baking powder
1 egg, lightly beaten

Cream the butter and sugar. Add the almonds and egg; beat until fluffy. Add the cinnamon, orange zest and rum; beat until smooth. In a separate bowl, stir together the flour and baking powder. Add to the butter mixture and combine lightly. Wrap the dough in plastic and refrigerate about one hour, until firm. Roll out the dough on a lightly floured surface to ¹/₄-inch thickness; cut out stars or other favorite shapes. Place cookies ¹/₂-inch apart on greased baking sheet. Brush the cookies with the beaten egg and bake at 350 degrees for about 10 minutes, until light golden in color. After these cookies are completely cooled, store them in an airtight container. Makes 6 to 7 dozen.

## MAMOUL

*This is the first cookie I remember my grandmother making for special occasions. Every Christmas, I prepare a special tin for my dad with these cookies. He always says, "They taste just like Mama's."*

2 c. butter
2¹/₂ c. sugar, divided
6 c. all-purpose flour
1 c. milk, lukewarm
3 c. ground walnuts
1 t. orange-flower water
powdered sugar

Mix butter, 1¹/₂ cups sugar and flour, using your hands, if necessary. Add milk; mix with a wooden spoon.

Roll this mixture on a well-floured pastry cloth and cut into circles. In a mixing bowl, combine walnuts, remaining sugar and orange-flower water; set aside. Place spoonfuls of filling in the center of each pastry circle; fold in half and pinch edges. Place on a lightly greased baking sheet and bake at 350 degrees for 15 to 25 minutes. Cool on a rack; sprinkle with powdered sugar. Makes 6 to 7 dozen cookies, depending on the size.

*Antoinette Abdo-Whelpton*
*Scottsville, NY*

## FRUITCAKE COOKIES

My very good friend gave several dozen of these cookies to us one Christmas, all wrapped so prettily. Of course, we enjoyed the cookies so much, I asked for the recipe and have used it many times since over the years. Excellent for Christmas gift giving or holiday parties, since they freeze well. You may halve the recipe if 16 dozen is too many!

1 c. brown sugar, packed
1 c. margarine, melted
3 eggs
3 c. all-purpose flour
1 t. baking soda
1 t. cinnamon
7 c. chopped nuts
$1/2$ c. milk
12 oz. candied pineapple
8-oz. pkg. candied red cherries
8-oz. pkg. candied green cherries
2  8-oz. pkgs. dates
15-oz. box golden raisins

Combine brown sugar and margarine. Add eggs. Combine dry ingredients alternately with milk. Stir fruit and nuts into dough (you may have to use your hands to mix dough at this point, because it's VERY stiff). Drop by heaping teaspoonfuls onto well-greased baking sheets and bake at 300 degrees for 20 minutes. Makes about 16 dozen.

*Kim Breuer*

*These little Fruitcake Cookies are big on flavor! A rustic painted Shaker box (how-to's on page 128) is perfect for toting them to the office or to a party.*

## CHOCOLATE GINGERBREAD COOKIES

*Easy and delightful!*

$1/2$ c. molasses
$1/4$ c. sugar
3 T. butter
1 T. milk
2 c. all-purpose flour
$1/2$ t. baking soda
$1/2$ t. nutmeg
$1/2$ t. cinnamon
$1/2$ t. ground cloves
$1/2$ t. ground ginger
3 T. water

Heat molasses to boiling. Reduce heat to medium and add sugar, butter and milk; stir until butter melts. In a large bowl, mix dry ingredients with molasses mixture and water; blend well. Roll to $1/4$-inch thickness and cut with your favorite cookie cutter. Lightly spray baking sheet with non-stick vegetable spray. Bake at 350 degrees for 6 to 8 minutes.

Icing:
1 c. chocolate bits, melted
$1/3$ c. warm milk

Stir chocolate bits and warm milk together until smooth; spread over cookies.

*Mildred Bright*
*Riverdale, MD*

# Make it a Mix!

*When you need the perfect gift but don't have a lot of time, make it a mix! Help a busy mom make a no-fuss meal with our soup starter or chili mix, or treat a midnight snacker to the fixings for chocolatey brownies and spiced cider. We've even got festive ideas the kids can make and give!*

*Treat a friend to tea with a prettily trimmed basket (see page 128) packed with Friendship Scone Mix. Include a batch of freshly baked scones for her to enjoy right away!*

## FRIENDSHIP SCONE MIX

*Substitute ¹/₂ cup sweetened, dried cranberries or ¹/₂ teaspoon orange zest in place of the mini chocolate chips for variety.*

1³/₄ c. all-purpose flour
1 T. baking powder
¹/₂ t. salt
1 c. quick-cooking oats, uncooked
¹/₂ c. chopped walnuts
¹/₃ c. mini semi-sweet chocolate chips

Combine first 3 ingredients in a large mixing bowl; stir in remaining ingredients. Mix well. Store in an airtight container in a cool, dry place. Makes 3¹/₂ cups mix. Attach the following instructions:
Place scone mix in a large mixing bowl; cut in ¹/₂ cup butter until mixture resembles coarse crumbs. In a separate bowl, whisk ¹/₄ cup milk with one egg. Add to crumb mixture; stir just until moistened. Knead gently on a lightly floured surface 8 to 10 times; pat dough into an 8-inch circle on a lightly greased baking sheet. Cut into 8 wedges; do not separate. Bake at 375 degrees until golden, about 10 to 12 minutes. Cut wedges again and serve warm. Makes 8.

## COCONUT BROWNIE MIX

*These brownies are full of goodies that everyone will enjoy!*

¹/₃ c. chopped walnuts
¹/₂ c. chocolate chips
¹/₃ c. flaked coconut
²/₃ c. brown sugar, packed
³/₄ c. sugar
¹/₃ c. baking cocoa
1¹/₂ c. all-purpose flour

Layer ingredients in a one-quart, wide-mouth jar. Pack each layer down as tightly as possible before adding the next layer. Copy and color the gift tag (page 155); write instructions on back of the tag: Add brownie mix to 2 eggs, ²/₃ cup oil and 1 teaspoon vanilla extract. Blend well. Spread in greased 8"x8" baking dish. Bake at 350 degrees for 30 minutes or until center tests done. Makes one dozen.

Carol Weimer
Saltsburg, PA

## APPLE CIDER SPICE MIX

*Make several of these mixes to have on hand for giving.*

2 c. sugar
2 t. cinnamon
1 t. ground cloves
1¹/₂ t. ground allspice
¹/₄ t. nutmeg

Combine ingredients; store in an airtight container. Makes about 24 servings. Give mix with a jug of apple cider and instructions: Heat one cup cider until hot but not boiling; stir in 2 teaspoons cider mix until dissolved. Pour into a serving mug; garnish with a cinnamon stick and slice of orange.

Annette Ingram
Grand Rapids, MI

For a winter warmer, fill a basket with a jug of apple cider, spiced cider mix, mugs, coasters, oranges and a bunch of cinnamon sticks tied up with a pretty ribbon.

*Bake up a batch of moist Coconut Brownies for the neighbors and include a jar of the layered mix, too! Write the baking instructions on a separate piece of card stock and tie to the hand-tinted gift tag.*

### Love Thy Neighbor...

give her a pretty jar of

### Italian Pasta Fagiola Soup Mix

Rinse beans in cold water and sort out shriveled ones. Dry on paper towels overnight and combine with spices listed in recipe below. Layer beans in a mason jar for a pretty presentation. Package the pasta in a separate package or jar, and add a photocopy of the "How To" for a tasty gift, page 157.

### Bean & Spice Mix:

³/₄ c. dried Great Northern Beans
³/₄ c. pinto beans
³/₄ c. red beans
¹/₄ c. dried minced onion
2 t. dried minced garlic
1 t. dried oregano
1 bay leaf

1 t. dried basil
¹/₂ t. dried celery flakes
¹/₂ t. dried rosemary
³/₄ t. salt
¹/₈ t. crushed red pepper
1¹/₄ c. small pasta (shells, bowties or ditalini)

## CINNAMON-SPICE SPRINKLE

*Add to sliced fruit, pudding and in muffin cups before adding batter.*

10 T. sugar, divided
1 t. cinnamon
1 t. ground ginger
1 t. cardamom
1 t. coriander
1 t. nutmeg

Layer spices into a one-cup narrow, clear jar. Makes about ³/₄ cup. Give with instructions to shake mixture gently until well blended.

## CAJUN SPICE MIX

*Sprinkle this on eggs, potatoes and meat dishes...yum!*

²/₃ c. salt, divided
¹/₄ c. cayenne pepper, divided
2 T. white pepper
2 T. pepper
2 T. paprika
2 T. onion powder
2 T. garlic powder

Layer in a pint jar in desired order, dividing salt and cayenne pepper into several layers. Makes 1¹/₂ cups.

## JOLLY HOLIDAYS JAR COOKIES

*Make 'em, bake 'em and share 'em!*

¹/₄ c. sugar
¹/₂ c. brown sugar, packed
1¹/₂ c. all-purpose flour
³/₄ t. baking soda
¹/₂ t. baking powder
¹/₂ c. mini green and red candy-coated chocolates
¹/₂ c. quick-cooking oats, uncooked
¹/₂ c. cocoa crispy rice cereal
¹/₂ c. white chocolate chips

Layer the ingredients in a one-quart, wide-mouth jar in the order listed; pack down each layer firmly. Tighten the lid and attach the following instructions: Cream together ¹/₂ cup butter or margarine, one teaspoon vanilla extract and one egg in a large mixing bowl; add cookie mix, stirring until well blended. Drop by teaspoonfuls onto ungreased baking sheets; bake at 350 degrees for 10 to 12 minutes. Makes about 4 dozen.

*Tonya Sheppard*
*Galveston, TX*

## SPICY WINTER TeA MIX

a recipe from Patti Davis ★ Kiowa, OK

1·¼ c. orange drink mix
3/4 c. sweetened instant tea
½ t. ground cloves
½ t. allspice
.23-oz. pkg. lemonade drink mix
1 t. cinnamon
3-oz. pkg. apricot gelatin
9-oz. pkg. red cinnamon candies

Combine all ingredients together and store in an airtight container. Makes about 3·½ cups dry mix.

### ☆ A Packaging Idea! ☆

Visit your neighborhood craft store for a stack of small clay pots ～ they're great country·style containers that, with a coat of paint, will carry your tea mix with down·home flair. Simply paint the pots a dark red or forest green; rub a bit of the color off with fine sandpaper when dry. Stencil a star and the word "TeA" on the pots, or use rubber stamps to decorate the pots. Package the tea mix in zip·lock bags and gather a piece of muslin or plaid homespun fabric around the mix ～ tie shut with raffia or twine and place in the painted pots. Add photocopy of directions, page 156!

## PARTY DILL DIP BLEND

*Include this seasoning mix with a round loaf of pumpernickel for an instant party!*

½ c. dill weed
½ c. dried, minced onion
½ c. dried parsley
¼ t. celery seed
1 T. paprika
1 T. garlic powder
1 T. dried thyme
2 t. celery salt

Combine ingredients; store in an airtight container. Makes about 2 cups. Give with the following instructions: Whisk 3 tablespoons mix with one cup mayonnaise and one cup sour cream. Refrigerate at least one to 2 hours before serving. Makes about 2½ cups.

## GO-TEAM CHILI SEASONING

*Give this seasoning mix with a stack of soup bowls or a new stockpot...just right for a winter evening.*

1 T. all-purpose flour
2 T. dried, minced onion
1½ t. chili powder
1 t. salt
½ t. cayenne pepper
½ t. garlic powder
1 t. sugar
½ t. cumin

Mix all ingredients together; store in an airtight container. Makes ½ cup. Give mix and the following instructions: Brown one pound ground beef in a skillet; drain. Add seasoning mix, two 15½-ounce cans kidney beans and two 16-ounce cans stewed tomatoes. Reduce heat; simmer for 10 minutes, stirring occasionally. Makes 4 to 6 servings.

# Snowflake Muffin Mix

a 'specially yummy recipe from Linda Hensz ✶ Beach Lake, PA

These are oh-so-fragrant and good on a snowy day! Pack a disposable plastic container with this mix... tie on a paper snowflake with a blue satin ribbon... and pull on your snowboots and deliver to a friendly neighbor!

2 c. all-purpose flour
1 T. dry onion soup mix
1½ T. sugar
2 t. baking powder
½ t. baking soda
¼ t. salt

Measure ingredients in a medium mixing bowl; stir and store in an airtight container.

*Seasoned with onion soup mix, savory Snowflake Muffins are great served with hearty winter soups or stews. Pack a bag of muffin mix, along with a handful of paper liners, in a snowflake container (instructions on page 129).*

# Merry Mixes from little hands

Here are FUN little recipes for kids in the kitchen... easy to make, and not a one has to be precise... so what if Frosty's Toppers is 99% gumdrops? Your little elves will have a holiday blast mixing up gifts for neighbors, Aunt Helen and the mailman, too. So get out the crayons, color the tags and get mixin'!

*Don't stop the fun...after the kids have finished in the kitchen, let them tag their mixes with fun labels using bright chenille stems, beads and oversize sequins.* *Turn to page 129 for the kids' tags how-to's.*

## REINDEER TREATS

*Reindeer need their veggies, too, you know. Deliver to every neighbor's house where Rudolph stops by!*

**1 lb. bag peeled baby carrots**
**1 head cauliflower, divided into florets**

Combine carrots and cauliflower in plastic bags. Tie bags closed.

## FROSTY'S TOPPERS

*Use your imagination...fill a plastic bag with all kinds of yummy little candies to top off ice cream!*

**multicolored candy sprinkles**
**non-pareils**
**small candies**
**red and green gumdrops**
**mini marshmallows**
**peanuts**
**coconut**

Pour all ingredients into a mixing bowl. Your child can stir it up and spoon into individual plastic bags. Tie bags closed.

## SANTA SUGAR

*Yum! Santa will love this pretty sugar for his tea or cereal!*

**1 c. sugar**
**red and green colored sugar**
**star-shaped cookie sprinkles**

Pour ingredients into a mixing bowl. Stir together and spoon into individual bags. Tie bags closed.

## ELVES' SNACK MIX

*All Santa's elves need a snack during the busy holiday season! Use your favorite dried fruits, nuts and candies.*

**dried pineapple, cranberries, apricots,**
   **cherries and apples**
**raisins**
**coconut chips**
**red and green candy-coated chocolates**
**mini marshmallows**
**peanuts**
**red and green candy corn**

Combine ingredients in a bowl. Scoop into plastic bags. Tie bags closed.

## KIDS' KRUNCH

*Like most families, ours loves to have sweet munchies around to pick up by the handfuls. So, we concocted this creation without nuts and coconut just for the kids...no grown-up stuff allowed!*

1/2 c. margarine
1 c. brown sugar, packed
1/2 c. dark corn syrup
1 box bite-size crispy rice cereal
    squares

Melt margarine, sugar and corn syrup in a saucepan. Pour over cereal; toss well. Bake on a baking sheet or in a roasting pan at 250 degrees for one hour, stirring every 15 minutes. Pour on wax paper to cool. Store in an airtight container.

*Kim Estes*

## SNOWMAN SOUP

*A sweet & simple gift for kids and kids at heart!*

1-oz. pkg. hot cocoa mix
1 candy cane
2 T. mini marshmallows
1 milk chocolate drop

Place ingredients in a plastic zipping bag and attach instructions: Santa says you've been good this year...I'm always glad to hear it! With freezing weather drawing near, You'll need to warm the spirit. Here's a little snowman soup, Complete with stirring stick. Add hot water and sip it slow...it's sure to do the trick!

*Sandra Renaux*
*Orlando, FL*

*Bake a batch of brightly decorated cookies and share them with the cooks in your child's cafeteria. They'll appreciate the treat from your kitchen!*

*— Tami Bowman*
*Gooseberry Patch*

*Here's a neat idea for classroom gifts: Tuck single-serving bags of chocolatey Snowman Soup mix in wintry mugs and add peppermint canes for stirring. To decorate the mugs and make the tags, see page 129.*

# North Pole Cookie Bar Mix
### ...a little elf's favorite!

a recipe from Zoe Bennett Columbia, SC

1/2 c. oats, uncooked
1/2 c. raspberry chips
1 c. brown sugar, packed & divided

2 c. buttermilk biscuit baking mix, divided

In a wide-mouth, one-quart glass jar, layer ingredients in this order. Oats, raspberry chips, 1/2 cup brown sugar, one cup buttermilk biscuit baking mix, 1/2 cup brown sugar and one cup buttermilk biscuit baking mix. Pack layers in jar tightly, and if there's room left, add more chips to top of jar. Give with instructions, page 157.

85

# Festive FARE

Whenever family & friends gather to celebrate, there's sure to be laughter and cheer...and of course, lots of wonderful things to eat! Our Gooseberry Patch friends have gathered an outstanding collection of festive fare, from tasty tidbits to savory entrées, sensational sides and heavenly desserts and sweets! You'll find quick dishes for family meals and entertaining, as well as lots of breakfast goodies. Grab your fork and dig in!

*For a traditional feast, baste Roast Turkey with sage butter for extra flavor; serve with savory Gravy. Sensational sides include Sweet Potato Pudding and Green Beans Supreme (recipes on pages 90 and 91).*

# The BEST Christmas Dinner Ever

*Gather everyone 'round the table to enjoy the best Yuletide dinner ever! We've got a great selection, from savory starters to your choice of roast turkey or pork…and of course, scrumptious desserts.*

*Smoked Salmon Canapés, Citrus and Spice Punch, Veggie Puffs*

## VEGGIE PUFFS

*You can also fill these with sweet potato, cheese, or try any of your favorite fillings!*

16   4-inch sqs. puff pastry dough
1 1/2 to 2 c. frozen mixed broccoli,
    carrots and cauliflower
3 egg whites, divided
1/4 c. shredded mozzarella cheese
1/4 c. shredded Cheddar cheese
1/8 t. dried basil
Garnish: sesame seeds

Defrost puff pastry dough squares for 5 to 10 minutes. Cook vegetables according to package directions; mash. Beat 2 egg whites and add to vegetables. Blend in cheeses and basil; mix well. Place one tablespoon filling in the center of each dough square. Fold dough to form triangles. Using the tines of a fork, seal edges of the dough. Lightly beat the third egg white and brush the top of the dough; sprinkle with sesame seeds. Place on a lightly oiled baking sheet and bake at 375 degrees for 12 to 15 minutes.

Marissa Charyton
North Bellimore, NY

## SMOKED SALMON CANAPÉS

*For casual gatherings or fancy parties, everyone loves salmon!*

1 c. sour cream
1/4 t. lemon zest, finely grated
1 loaf of party-size light rye bread
4 T. unsalted butter, melted
1/2 lb. smoked salmon, sliced and
    cut into strips
2 scallions, thinly sliced

Combine the sour cream and lemon zest and chill for 2 hours. Brush the bread slices with butter and cut each slice in half diagonally. Arrange the bread triangles on baking sheets and bake at 350 degrees for about 10 minutes, or until lightly toasted. Let cool completely. Spoon chilled lemon cream on top of each toast. Place a salmon strip on top and garnish with scallions.

What a wonderful time of year! Toast the season with a cup of delicious

# Citrus and Spice PUNCH

**★ SPICE MIX**

1-½ c. WATER
½ c. SUGAR
3 CINNAMON STICKS, BROKEN
1 t. WHOLE ALLSPICE
½ t. WHOLE CLOVES

Place ingredients in a saucepan ∽simmer, covered, for 20 minutes. Strain out spices. Chill.

**★ FRUIT JUICE MIX**

6-oz. CAN FROZEN ORANGE JUICE CONCENTRATE
6-oz. CAN FROZEN PINEAPPLE JUICE CONCENTRATE
2½ c. WATER
¼ c. LEMON OR LIME JUICE
1 QT. GINGER ALE

Blend juices and WATER together. Combine with spice mixture in punch bowl. Add ice ring & ginger ale.

— ★ —

*A BIG OLD CROCK BOWL MAKES A GOOD COUNTRY PUNCH BOWL.*

## Decorative Ice Ring

★ Fluted ring mold or decorative metal mold
★ Slices of lemon, lime, orange or pineapple
★ red or green cherries
★ raspberries, cranberries, blueberries or strawberries
★ mint leaves
★ extra juice or ginger ale used in punch recipe

Arrange desired fruit in bottom of mold. Fill with juice or soda. Place in freezer 'til completely frozen. To unmold, wrap a hot towel around mold to release ice ring. Place in punch bowl.

## FESTIVE CHEESE BALL

*Make ahead of time to allow flavors to blend.*

2 8-oz. pkgs. cream cheese, softened
2 c. shredded Cheddar cheese
1 T. onion, finely chopped
1 T. pimento, finely chopped
1 T. green pepper, finely chopped
2 t. Worcestershire sauce
1 t. lemon juice
⅛ t. salt
⅛ t. cayenne pepper
½ c. chopped walnuts
crackers

In a medium bowl, blend cheeses together with a fork. Mix in remaining ingredients except the walnuts and crackers. Place mixture on plastic wrap and shape into a ball; chill thoroughly. Roll in chopped walnuts and serve with crackers. Makes 4 cups.

Sonia Schork
Lakeside, AZ

*From the time my husband and I have had the family Christmas dinner (30 years+), we have always had a small, wrapped gift or favor for each member to open at the table before dinner. It is a fun "together" time, and everyone has a good feeling.*

*— Marjorie Foland*
*Wilmington, OH*

## WILD RICE SOUP

*For a special touch, top with crispy homemade croutons and crumbled bacon.*

1¹/₃ c. chicken broth
1¹/₂ c. quick-cooking wild rice, uncooked
1 lb. sliced bacon, cooked and crumbled, drippings reserved
1 onion, chopped
2  10³/₄-oz. cans cream of potato soup
2  4.5-oz. jars sliced mushrooms, undrained
2 c. half-and-half
²/₃ c. sharp pasteurized process cheese spread

Bring chicken broth to a boil; add rice. Cover, reduce heat and simmer 5 minutes or until liquid is absorbed. Spoon bacon drippings into a saucepan and sauté onion. Reserve ¹/₃ cup crumbled bacon for topping. Stir in remaining ingredients and rice. Heat, but don't boil. Sprinkle each serving with croutons and reserved bacon. Makes 12 cups.

Gail Saucier
Mankato, MN

## CRANBERRY-GLAZED PORK ROAST

*Serve pork for the New Year…it's good luck!*

4-lb. boneless pork loin roast
2 t. cornstarch
¹/₄ t. cinnamon
¹/₈ t. salt
¹/₂ t. orange zest
2 T. orange juice
16 oz. whole berry cranberry sauce

In a small saucepan, stir together all ingredients except pork. Cook, stirring over medium heat until thickened. Place roast in shallow baking dish. Roast at 325 degrees for 45 minutes. Spoon ¹/₂ cup glaze over roast and continue roasting for 30 to 45 minutes or until a meat thermometer reads 155 to 160 degrees. Let stand 10 minutes before slicing and serve with remaining sauce. Serves 16.

Doris Stegner
Gooseberry Patch

## GREEN BEANS SUPREME

*This isn't your usual green bean casserole. Loaded with cheese and sour cream, it will be your new favorite!*

1 onion, sliced
1 T. fresh parsley, snipped
3 T. butter, divided
2 T. all-purpose flour
¹/₂ t. lemon zest
¹/₂ t. salt
¹/₈ t. pepper
¹/₂ c. milk
8-oz. container sour cream
16-oz. pkg. frozen French-style green beans, cooked
¹/₂ c. shredded Cheddar cheese
¹/₄ c. fresh bread crumbs

Cook onion slices and parsley in 2 tablespoons butter until onion is tender. Blend in flour, lemon zest, salt and pepper. Stir in milk; heat until thick and bubbly. Add sour cream and beans; heat through. Spoon into an ungreased 2-quart baking dish; sprinkle with cheese. Melt remaining butter and toss with bread crumbs; sprinkle on top of beans. Broil 3 to 4 inches from heat source for 3 minutes or until golden. Makes 4 to 6 servings.

SueMary Burford-Smith
Tulsa, OK

*Wild Rice Soup, Riviera Salad*

## ROAST TURKEY & GRAVY

*A time-tested recipe that's become a holiday tradition.*

8 slices of bacon, crisply cooked and crumbled
1 c. unsalted butter, softened
3 T. fresh sage, chopped
14-lb. turkey
salt and pepper to taste
3 leeks, white and green parts, chopped
8 fresh sage sprigs
3 bay leaves, crumbled
4 1/2 c. canned chicken broth
Garnish: fresh sage, parsley, bay leaves and pears

In a medium bowl, mix bacon, butter and sage. Season lightly with salt and pepper; set aside. Pat turkey dry with paper towels and season cavity with salt and pepper. Place leeks, sage and bay leaves in cavity. Loosen skin on turkey breast and spread 1/3 cup sage butter over meat, under skin. Place turkey on rack set in large roasting pan; rub 2 tablespoons sage butter over outside of turkey. Set aside 1/3 cup butter for gravy; reserve remaining for basting. Position rack in bottom third of oven and preheat to 350 degrees. Pour 1/3 cup broth over turkey and roast turkey at 350 degrees until thermometer inserted into meaty part of thigh registers 180 degrees. Baste every 30 minutes with 1/3 cup broth and brush with sage butter for approximately 3 hours. Transfer turkey to platter and let stand 30 minutes. To prepare gravy, pour pan juices back into saucepan, add 2 cups broth and bring to a boil. Continue to boil until liquid is reduced to 2 cups, about 10 minutes. Whisk in reserved 1/3 cup sage butter or to taste. Garnish with sage, parsley, bay leaves and pears.

*Vickie*

## RIVIERA SALAD

*A colorful salad...so pretty on a holiday buffet table.*

1/4 c. pecan halves
1 T. sugar
1/2 head Romaine lettuce, torn
1/2 head iceberg lettuce, torn
1/4 c. red onion, thinly sliced
1 c. strawberries, sliced
1/2 c. mayonnaise
1/4 c. half-and-half
1/2 c. sugar
1/4 c. cider vinegar
1 to 2 T. poppy seed

Combine pecans and sugar in a skillet over medium heat, stirring constantly, until the nuts are golden. Spread mixture on wax paper to cool; set aside. Toss together Romaine and iceberg lettuce; add onion, strawberries, and nuts. Whisk remaining ingredients and pour over salad. Makes 6 to 8 servings.

*Mary Schmidt*
*Bangor, WI*

## SWEET POTATO PUDDING

*This recipe has been in my family as long as I can remember! Every holiday, I get requests to bring this pudding.*

10 sweet potatoes, baked, peeled and mashed
3/4 c. brown sugar, packed
1/2 c. butter
4 eggs, beaten
3/4 to 1 c. half-and-half
1 t. cinnamon

Place potatoes in a large bowl, beat in brown sugar and butter; mix well. Blend in eggs, half-and-half and cinnamon. Whip until well blended; pour into a 13"x9" baking dish. Bake at 350 degrees for 30 to 40 minutes or until heated through. Makes 10 to 12 servings.

*Carolyn Celeste*
*Brick, NJ*

*"A small house well-filled is better than an empty palace."*

*— Thomas Haliburton*

# Nana's Waldorf Salad

MARY ELIZABETH REMEMBERS HER NANA WAS PARTICULARLY FOND OF FLOWERED HOUSEDRESSES, ORANGE CATS AND THIS DELICIOUS SALAD. "NANA ALWAYS ADDED CRANBERRIES TO THE DRESSING, WHICH MADE IT A PRETTY PINK COLOR ~ MY VERY FAVORITE!" SAYS MARY ELIZABETH.

INGREDIENTS:
2 c. CRISP APPLES, DICED
2 c. PEARS, DICED
1 c. RED & GREEN SEEDLESS GRAPES, HALVED

3/4 c. CELERY, SLICED
3/4 c. PECAN PIECES, TOASTED
1/2 c. WHOLE CRANBERRY SAUCE
1/4 c. MAYONNAISE
1/4 c. SOUR CREAM OR PLAIN YOGURT

3 T. MILK
2 t. LEMON JUICE
1 t. SUGAR

COMBINE FRUITS, CELERY & PECANS IN A BOWL. MIX REMAINING ITEMS FOR DRESSING. POUR OVER FRUIT & TOSS. CHILL 30 MINUTES BEFORE SERVING.

Make little bouquets of evergreen sprigs tied with festive ribbons and place one at each place setting at your holiday dinner table.

Wrap linen dinner napkins like little presents! Fold napkins into squares and trim with a bow...how clever!

## BUTTERY CRESCENT ROLLS

*These flaky crescents will melt in your mouth! Try them topped with homemade jam and real butter.*

1/2 c. milk
1/2 c. butter, softened
1/3 c. sugar
1/2 t. salt
1 pkg. active dry yeast
1/2 c. warm water
2 eggs, lightly beaten and divided
3 1/2 to 4 c. all-purpose flour

Heat milk until bubbles form; set aside. Blend together butter, sugar and salt; stir in hot milk and let mixture cool to lukewarm. Dissolve yeast in warm water; set aside for 5 to 10 minutes, then beat yeast mixture with one egg and stir into milk. Add 2 cups of flour and continue beating until mixture thickens. Stir in enough remaining flour until dough begins to pull away from the sides of the bowl. Knead dough on a lightly floured surface for 2 to 3 minutes. Place dough in an oiled bowl, turning once to coat. Let rise in a warm place until double in size, about one hour. Punch down dough and divide in half; let dough halves rest for 10 minutes. Roll one half of the dough into a 12-inch circle, cut each into 8 pie-shaped triangles. Beginning at large end, roll up each triangle. Place on a lightly oiled baking sheet and slightly curve ends to form crescent shape; repeat with remaining dough. Cover crescents and let rise again 30 minutes. Brush crescents with remaining beaten egg and bake at 400 degrees for 15 minutes. Yield 16 rolls.

*Robin Hill*
*Rochester, NY*

## PASTA CON BROCCOLI

*I remember both Mom & Dad in the kitchen preparing holiday meals...Mom roasting the turkey and Dad making this recipe. Finally, when dinner was ready, we'd all gather around an old oak table to enjoy it together.*

1/2 c. onion, chopped
1 T. butter
2 T. oil
8-oz. can tomato sauce
1 c. water
1 t. Italian seasoning
salt to taste
1/8 t. pepper
1 lb. rigatoni, cooked and drained
1 lb. broccoli, cooked and drained
1 1/2 c. bread crumbs, buttered and browned
1/2 c. grated Parmesan cheese

Sauté onion in butter and oil. Add tomato sauce, water, seasoning, salt and pepper. Simmer for 10 minutes. On platter or large serving dish, place cooked rigatoni, top with broccoli, tomato sauce mixture, bread crumbs and Parmesan cheese. Serves 4 to 6.

*Anne Messier*
*Sacramento, CA*

## HOT FRUIT SALAD

*What an easy, warm, Christmasy way to serve fruit.*

20-oz. can chunky applesauce
15-oz. can pineapple chunks, drained
15-oz. can sliced peaches, drained
15-oz. can apricot halves, drained
11-oz. can mandarin oranges, drained
21-oz. can cherry pie filling
1/2 c. brown sugar, packed
1 t. cinnamon

Mix all together in a 13"x9" pan. Bake one hour at 350 degrees; serve warm.

*"Small cheer and great welcome makes a merry feast."*

*— William Shakespeare*

*Pasta con Broccoli, Buttery Crescent Rolls*

*Bûche de Noël*

## BÛCHE DE NOËL

*This traditional French cake resembles the Yule logs of long ago.*

**Cake:**
1 c. all-purpose flour
1 t. baking powder
¹/₄ t. salt
4 eggs, separated
³/₄ c. sugar, divided
¹/₃ cup water
1 t. vanilla extract
3 T. powdered sugar

Grease bottom and sides of a 15"x10" jellyroll pan. Line with wax paper; grease and flour. Combine flour, baking powder and salt; set aside. Beat egg whites at high speed with an electric mixer until foamy. Gradually add ¹/₄ cup sugar, 1 tablespoon at a time, beating until stiff peaks form and sugar dissolves, about 2 to 4 minutes; set aside. Beat egg yolks in a large mixing bowl at high speed, gradually adding ¹/₂ cup sugar; beat 5 minutes or until thick and pale. Add water and vanilla extract; beat well. Add flour mixture; beat just until blended. Fold in about ¹/₃ of egg white mixture. Gently fold in remaining egg white mixture. Spread batter evenly into prepared pan. Bake at 375 degrees for 10 minutes or until top springs back when lightly touched. Sift powdered sugar in a 15"x10" rectangle on a cloth. When cake is done, immediately loosen from sides of pan; turn out onto cloth. Peel off wax paper. Starting at narrow end, roll up cake and cloth together; cool completely on a wire rack, seam side down.

**Frosting:**
3³/₄ c. sifted powdered sugar
¹/₂ c. baking cocoa
6 T. milk
6 T. butter, softened

While cake cools, combine powdered sugar and cocoa in a large bowl. Add milk and butter to sugar mixture; beat at medium speed with an electric mixer until smooth. Unroll cake and remove towel. Spread half of frosting onto cake; carefully reroll. Cut a 1-inch-thick diagonal slice from one end of cake roll. Place cake roll on a serving plate, seam side down. Position slice against side of cake roll to resemble knot; use frosting to "glue" in place. Spread remaining frosting over cake and knot. Score frosting with tines of a fork to resemble tree bark. If frosting is soft, chill cake before serving.

**Garnish:**
8-oz. pkg. marzipan, divided
yellow food coloring
green food coloring
red food coloring
red cinnamon candies
powdered sugar

For snowman and leaf garnishes, tint a very small piece of marzipan yellow. Tint another portion green; leave remaining marzipan white. Roll out green marzipan to ¹/₈-inch thick and cut into leaves. Roll white marzipan into 2 large, 2 medium and 2 small balls to form 2 snowmen. Form the yellow marzipan into noses. Dip a toothpick into food coloring and press into snowmen to form eyes, mouths and buttons. Use small sticks for arms. Garnish cake with leaves and candies to resemble holly. Display snowmen with powdered sugar.

# Sweet inspirations

*Inspire sweet holiday memories with delectable confections…tempting chocolates, old-fashioned taffy, caramels and more.*

*White Confetti Fudge, Microwave Peanut Brittle*

## MICROWAVE PEANUT BRITTLE

*A microwave treat…homemade in minutes. How easy!*

1½ c. roasted peanuts
1 c. sugar
½ c. corn syrup
½ t. salt
1 T. butter
1 t. vanilla extract
1 t. baking soda

In a large microwave-safe bowl, mix peanuts, sugar, corn syrup and salt. Cook on high for 6 to 7 minutes; mixture should be bubbly and peanuts lightly browned. Quickly stir in butter and vanilla; cook 2 to 3 additional minutes. Add baking soda and stir quickly until mixture is foamy. Immediately pour onto a greased baking sheet. Let cool for 15 minutes or longer. Break into pieces and store in an airtight container. Makes 14 to 16 servings.

*Susie Montag
Richlands, NC*

## WHITE CONFETTI FUDGE

*I like to keep this fudge on hand…just to snack on.*

1½ lbs. white chocolate
14-oz. can sweetened condensed milk
⅛ t. salt
1 t. vanilla extract
½ c. red candied cherries, chopped
½ c. green candied cherries, chopped

Melt chocolate with milk in a heavy saucepan, stirring constantly. Remove from heat; stir in remaining ingredients. Spread evenly in a buttered, wax paper-lined, 8"x8" baking pan; chill until firm. Turn out onto a cutting board; cut into small squares. Makes 2 dozen.

*Angela Nichols
Mt. Airy, NC*

Dear Lord, Bless the big kids and the little, Bless whoever invented peanut brittle.

CANDY

## DARK CHOCOLATE CARAMELS
*Chewy and so chocolatey!*

1 1/2 c. whipping cream
1 1/4 c. honey
8 oz. bittersweet chocolate,
 finely chopped
1/2 c. sugar
1/2 c. brown sugar, packed
2 T. unsalted butter, softened
1 t. vanilla extract
vegetable oil

Blend together cream, honey, chocolate and sugars. Over medium heat, bring mixture to a boil. Continue cooking syrup, stirring constantly, until the temperature reaches the hard ball stage, or 250 to 268 degrees on a candy thermometer. Remove saucepan from heat and quickly stir in butter and vanilla. Pour caramel mixture into an 8"x8" metal baking pan lined with aluminum foil and coated with oil. Set aside to cool for 2 hours. When cool, slide aluminum foil from baking pan. Cut candy into squares with an oiled knife. Store squares between sheets of wax paper in a container with a tight fitting lid.

Audrey Lett
Newark, DE

*Saltwater Taffy*

## SALTWATER TAFFY
*The epitome of ooey gooey! Divide and add favorite flavorings and colors to make batches and batches for a rainbow of tastes.*

2 c. sugar
1 c. corn syrup
1 t. salt
1 1/2 c. water
2 T. butter
1/4 t. green food coloring
3/4 t. peppermint extract

Combine sugar, corn syrup, salt and water in a 2-quart saucepan; cook over medium-high heat, stirring constantly, until sugar dissolves. Heat mixture, without stirring, until it reaches the hard ball stage, or 260 degrees on a candy thermometer. Remove from heat; mix in remaining ingredients. Pour onto a lightly buttered 15"x10" jelly roll pan or marble slab; cool just until able to handle. Butter hands; gather taffy into a ball and pull.

Continue to pull until light in color and hard to pull; divide into fourths. Pull each fourth into a long rope about 1/2-inch thick; cut into one-inch pieces using buttered scissors. Wrap individually in wax paper. Makes 1 1/2 pounds.

Carol Burns
Gooseberry Patch

*"Eggnog is fine, fruitcake is dandy,
But the best part of Christmas
Is Christmas candy!"*

— Unknown

# Homemade ♥ Turtles

a recipe from
Donna Juliano

Crystal Lake, IL

3 c. semi-sweet chocolate chips
7-oz. jar marshmallow creme
14-oz. can sweetened condensed milk
1 t. vanilla extract
1 lb. chopped walnuts
40 caramels

\*

Combine chocolate chips, marshmallow creme & milk in a saucepan; stir over low heat 'til melted. Remove from heat ∾ stir in vanilla & walnuts. Slice each caramel into 6 equal pieces; fold in. Drop turtles by teaspoonfuls onto wax paper. Makes 2 to 3 dozen.

KATE

Casanova valued chocolate over champagne as an aphrodisiac.

## PARTY MINTS

*Make mints with green and red peppermint sticks for a colorful candy.*

**20-oz. pkg. white melting chocolate**
**6 peppermint sticks or candy canes, crushed**

Chop chocolate into pieces. Place 1/2 of pieces in a microwave-safe glass bowl. Watching carefully, microwave until soft enough to stir, about 2 to 3 minutes. Stir in 1/2 of crushed peppermint candy. Thinly spread mixture onto a wax paper-lined baking sheet. Freeze 5 to 10 minutes. When firm, break into pieces. Repeat with remaining bark and candy. Makes 1 1/2 pounds.

## BUTTERY CHOCOLATE–NUT TOFFEE

*Fill a vintage jar with this toffee, then tie on a homespun bow...a tasty gift from your kitchen!*

**1 c. butter**
**1 c. sugar**
**6-oz. pkg. semi-sweet chocolate chips**
**1/4 c. chopped walnuts**

In a 2-quart saucepan, combine butter and sugar. Cook over medium-low heat, stirring occasionally, until a small amount of the mixture dropped into ice water forms a brittle strand, or a candy thermometer reaches 300 degrees. Spread on wax paper-lined jelly roll pan. Sprinkle chocolate chips over hot candy; let stand 5 minutes. Spread melted chocolate evenly over candy; sprinkle with walnuts. Cool completely. Break into pieces.

Lynn Blamer
Bangor, MI

Make a sugarplum tree using a plastic foam cone! Place colorful gumdrops or other soft candies on toothpicks and insert into the foam until the tree is completely covered...a pretty decoration that's edible, too.

## CHOCOLATE SURPRISES

*You can also roll these truffle-like candies in sweet cocoa powder or grated coconut.*

6-oz. pkg. semi-sweet chocolate
   pieces
1/2 c. sour cream
1/4 t. salt, divided
24 vanilla wafers, crushed
2 1/2 T. rum or 1 t. rum extract
3 T. butter, melted
2 T. baking cocoa
1/2 c. powdered sugar
1/2 c. pecans or walnuts, finely
   chopped
2 3/4-oz. jar chocolate sprinkles

Melt chocolate pieces in top of double boiler over hot, not boiling, water. Remove from heat and stir in sour cream and 1/8 teaspoon salt. Refrigerate overnight. In small bowl, use a fork to mix vanilla wafer crumbs with rum, butter, cocoa, powdered sugar, nuts and remaining 1/8 teaspoon salt until mixture holds its shape easily. Form chilled chocolate mixture into balls the size of a grape. Coat each chocolate ball with the wafer-crumb mixture until it's the size of a walnut. Roll balls in chocolate sprinkles. Store in an airtight container in refrigerator for 24 hours to mellow. Makes 2 to 2 1/2 dozen.

## CANDY BALLS

*These nutty, fruit-filled candies are easy to make and they store well.*

2 c. graham cracker crumbs
6-oz. pkg. chopped, mixed dried
   fruit bits
1 c. pecans, chopped
14-oz. can sweetened condensed
   milk

Mix ingredients with a spoon or hands. Roll into balls the size of cherries. Store in the refrigerator with a sheet of waxed paper between each layer.

*Diane Dollak*
*Fair Haven, NJ*

## COCONUT JOYS

*My daughter and I love these...we can't get enough of them!*

1/2 c. margarine
2 c. powdered sugar
3 c. flaked coconut
2 1-oz. squares milk chocolate,
   melted
Garnish: finely chopped nuts

In a large saucepan, melt margarine; remove from heat. Add powdered sugar and coconut; mix well. Shape rounded teaspoonfuls into balls. Place balls on a parchment-lined baking sheet, then make indentations in the center of each. Fill indentations on each ball with chocolate; sprinkle nuts over chocolate, if desired. Chill 3 hours or until firm. Makes 3 dozen.

*Flo Burtnett*
*Gage, OK*

*Our concluding Christmas ritual occurs after the tree and decorations are put away...we make homemade vanilla ice cream! Using our leftover candy canes, we crush them and stir the candy into the ice cream just as it is finished. Of course, we make a real family project of turning the crank of the ice cream maker. "No turn, no eat!"*

*— Beth Krakowski*

*Homemade Turtles, Party Mints, Coconut Joys*

# Quick to Fix, Good to Eat

*Make your holidays almost hassle free...at least in the kitchen! From appetizers and snacks to main dishes and super sides, even desserts and goodies, these quick & easy recipes are a snap to prepare for family meals and treats for unexpected guests.*

*Bean & Pasta Soup*

## HOLIDAY PUNCH

*You can easily substitute your favorite color and flavor of gelatin.*

6-oz. pkg. cranberry gelatin
12-oz. can frozen lemonade
12-oz. can frozen orange juice
46-oz. can pineapple juice
2-ltr. bottle lemon-lime
   carbonated soda

Blend together gelatin, lemonade, orange juice and pineapple juice until gelatin is dissolved; stir in soda and serve.

Bonnie Egenton
Hillsborough, NJ

## BAKED SWEET ONION SPREAD

*Try this spread on crackers, toast points or pita chips. It's a slightly sweet, cheesy spread that's sure to become a new favorite for family and friends!*

1 sweet onion, chopped
1 c. grated Parmesan cheese
1 c. mayonnaise
1/8 t. garlic salt
1/8 t. lemon juice

Mix all ingredients well. Spread in a one-quart baking dish and bake at 350 degrees for 10 minutes or until warm throughout. Serves 6.

Valerie Sheppard
Valdosta, GA

## BEAN & PASTA SOUP

*Fill several insulated containers with this terrific soup and hitch up the wagon for a winter hayride!*

2 T. olive oil
2 zucchini, cut in half lengthwise
    and thickly sliced
1/2 t. dried basil leaves, crushed
1/4 t. garlic powder
2 10 1/2-oz. cans condensed
    chicken broth
2 14 1/2-oz. cans diced tomatoes,
    undrained
1/2 c. elbow or twist macaroni,
    uncooked
15-oz. can kidney beans, rinsed
    and drained
Garnish: grated Parmesan cheese

Over medium heat, heat oil in a 4-quart saucepan. Add zucchini, basil and garlic powder and cook until vegetables are crisp-tender. Add broth, one soup can full of water and tomatoes. Heat to boiling. Add macaroni. Reduce heat to low. Cook 10 minutes or until macaroni is tender, stirring occasionally. Add beans. Heat through, stirring occasionally. Sprinkle with cheese and serve.

*Sandy Spayer*
*Jeromesville, OH*

## COMFORT SOUP

*Add your favorite vegetables or cheese to this soup!*

10-oz. pkg. frozen, chopped
    broccoli, thawed
10 1/2-oz. can cream of potato
    soup
1 c. milk
1 c. shredded Cheddar cheese

In a large microwave-safe dish, heat broccoli. Add soup, milk and cheese; stir. Heat in microwave until hot and cheese is melted. Makes 3 to 4 servings.

*Jan Berry*
*Woodridge, IL*

## RED BANDANNA STEW

*A slow cooker makes this dish a low-fuss meal for families on the go.*

1 lb. ground beef, browned
2 15-oz. cans new potatoes,
    drained and chopped
8 1/4-oz. can sliced carrots, drained
1 1/4-oz. pkg. taco seasoning mix
1/2 c. water
1 c. picante sauce
1 c. shredded Cheddar cheese

Place browned beef in a slow cooker; add potatoes and carrots. In a separate mixing bowl, combine taco seasoning with water; pour into slow cooker. Cook on high setting about 30 minutes to one hour; garnish with picante sauce and cheese. Serves 4 to 6.

*Doni Boothe*
*Magnolia, TX*

## ZESTY SALSA & CHEESE BREAD

*This is one of my favorite family recipes...enjoy!*

10-oz. tube refrigerated pizza
    crust
8-oz. jar salsa
garlic salt to taste
8-oz. pkg. shredded Cheddar
    cheese
8-oz. pkg. shredded mozzarella
    cheese

Spread pizza crust on lightly greased baking sheet. Spread salsa down the middle of the pizza crust. Sprinkle salsa with garlic salt and cheeses. Bring edges of pizza crust to middle, leaving approximately one inch open. Bake at 375 degrees for 15 to 20 minutes or until cheese is melted and crust is golden. Slice and serve warm. Serves 4.

*Cheryl Wilson*
*Coshocton, OH*

---

### the QUICK-COOKER'S PANTRY

...GOT 'EM?

☐ BROTH ~ BEEF & CHICKEN
☐ BOUILLON CUBES
☐ BREAD CRUMBS, REGULAR OR SEASONED
☐ CANNED TUNA & CHICKEN
☐ CANNED TOMATOES & TOMATO SAUCE, NO SALT & SEASONED VARIETIES
☐ CANNED BEANS
☐ CAKE & QUICK BREAD MIXES
☐ CONDIMENTS ~ SALSA, SOY SAUCE, HOT PEPPER SAUCE, HONEY, HORSERADISH, KETCHUP, MUSTARDS
☐ SOUP ~ CANNED & DRY MIXES
☐ PASTA ~ ALL SHAPES & SAUCES
☐ PEANUT BUTTER
☐ RICE ~ REGULAR, INSTANT & DON'T FORGET BROWN!
☐ OATMEAL
☐ SEASONINGS ~ HERBS, SPICES & GARLIC
☐ READY-MADE PASTA SAUCES
☐ WALNUTS, PECANS & ALMONDS
☑ CHOCOLATE CHIPS
☐ VINEGARS

...one out of eighteen... is that bad?

---

*A*dd a tangy twist to bean soup by drizzling
some balsamic vinegar in while it simmers.

## LEMON-BROILED SALMON

*This cooks quickly, making it perfect for a holiday brunch.*

4 salmon steaks
1/2 c. butter, melted
salt and pepper to taste
2 t. fresh dill weed, chopped
2 t. fresh parsley, chopped
juice of one lemon

Brush each salmon steak with one tablespoon butter; set aside. Blend remaining butter with salt, pepper, dill weed, parsley and lemon juice. Place salmon under broiler and broil 5 minutes; turn. Brush on butter mixture, then broil the second side for 5 minutes. Makes 4 servings.

*Tori Willis*
*Champaign, IL*

## ORANGE-MAPLE GLAZED CARROTS

*This dish always impresses guests…don't let them know you did it in the microwave.*

2/3 c. orange juice
16-oz. pkg. peeled baby carrots
zest of one orange
1/3 c. maple syrup
1 t. fresh nutmeg, grated
1/3 c. butter

Heat orange juice in a microwave-safe casserole dish in the microwave on high for 1 1/2 minutes. Add carrots and orange zest; stir to coat. Cover dish and microwave on high for 7 minutes. Stir in the remaining ingredients and microwave, uncovered, for 2 minutes. Carrots should be crisp-tender; if not, microwave an additional 2 minutes. Makes 3 to 4 servings.

*Elizabeth Blackstone*
*Racine, WI*

*Super-quick apple punch! Combine four cups of cider with one quart vanilla ice cream and two cups of lemon-lime soda.*

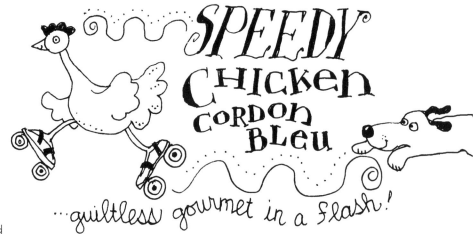

# SPEEDY Chicken Cordon Bleu

*…guiltless gourmet in a flash!*

1 T. Margarine
4 Chicken breast halves, boneless & skinless
10 3/4-oz. can cream of Chicken soup
1/2 c. shredded Swiss cheese

1/4 lb. cooked ham slices
1/4 c. white wine
8-oz. pkg. noodles, uncooked

Melt margarine in a large skillet. Cook chicken until brown on both sides ~ about 10 minutes. Remove from pan and keep warm. In the same skillet, combine soup and cheese. Cut sliced ham into thin strips. Add ham and white wine to soup mixture in skillet. Bring to a boil, stirring constantly. Return chicken to skillet. Over low heat, cover and cook 8 to 10 minutes or until chicken is no longer pink. In the meantime, cook noodles according to package directions. Drain. Serve chicken on bed of hot cooked noodles.

*Speedy Chicken Cordon Bleu, Orange-Maple Glazed Carrots*

## WILD RICE SALAD
*A great way to use leftover holiday turkey.*

4 c. fresh spinach, torn
2 c. turkey, cooked and cubed
2 c. wild rice, cooked
1 onion, chopped
1 c. fresh mushrooms, sliced
20 cherry tomatoes, halved
8-oz. bottle Italian dressing

Combine spinach, turkey, rice, onion, mushrooms and tomatoes. When ready to serve, toss with dressing.

Angela Murphy
Tempe, AZ

*Wild Rice Salad, Easy Rolls*

Home ★ Breads
IN A
★ SNAP ★

who's got time to make homemade bread? You do! Try our recipes!

EASY ROLLS
★★★★★★ ★★★★★★★★

2 c. SELF-RISING FLOUR
4 T. MAYONNAISE
1 c. MILK
1 t. SUGAR

MIX ALL TOGETHER IN MEDIUM MIXING BOWL. SPOON INTO 12 LIGHTLY-GREASED MUFFIN CUPS. BAKE AT 425° FOR 16 TO 18 MINUTES.

OLD ★ TIMEY CORNBREAD ★★★

MIX THIS UP & KEEP ON HAND IN THE PANTRY FOR QUICK-BAKING BREAD!
★
9 c. ALL-PURPOSE FLOUR    4 T. BAKING
3 c. YELLOW CORNMEAL        POWDER
4 t. SALT                           3 c. SUGAR

MIX ALL TOGETHER WITH A WIRE WHISK IN LARGE BOWL. STORE IN AIRTIGHT CONTAINER AT ROOM TEMPERATURE. WHEN READY TO MAKE BREAD FOLLOW THESE QUICK INSTRUCTIONS:

3.3/4 c. CORNBREAD MIX
2 EGGS, BEATEN
1.1/2 c. MILK
2 T. MARGARINE, MELTED

PLACE MIX IN BOWL. MAKE WELL IN CENTER FOR LIQUID INGREDIENTS. COMBINE EGGS & MILK ~ POUR INTO WELL IN MIX CENTER. ADD MELTED BUTTER. STIR 'TIL MOISTENED, BUT DO NOT OVERMIX. BAKE IN WELL-GREASED BREAD PAN (9" SQUARE IS GOOD) FOR 35 TO 45 MINUTES OR UNTIL WOODEN PICK INSERTED IN CENTER COMES OUT CLEAN.

## DOZEN EGG CORN CASSEROLE
*Feed the gang well before a day of shopping!*

12 eggs, beaten
2 17-oz. cans cream-style corn
4 c. shredded sharp Cheddar cheese
2 4-oz. cans chopped green chilies, drained
1 T. salt
1 T. Worcestershire sauce
1/2 t. pepper

Preheat oven to 325 degrees. In large bowl, combine all ingredients and beat until well mixed. Pour into 13"x9" baking dish. This can be prepared ahead of time. Cover and refrigerate up to 24 hours. Bake one hour and 15 minutes or until firm to touch. Makes 6 to 8 servings.

## CABBAGE & PORK CHOP CASSEROLE
*For this old-fashioned recipe, I usually don't even measure the ingredients, I just keep adding them until it "looks right!"*

4 pork chops
1 T. oil
10³/₄-oz. can cream of celery soup
1/2 c. milk
1/2 head of cabbage, shredded
6 potatoes, sliced

Brown pork chops in oil, remove to plate. Add soup and milk to pork chop drippings, stirring well. Bring to a simmer and cook until soup and milk are well blended. Place cabbage on the bottom of a 13"x9" pan. Lay pork chops on top of cabbage. Layer potatoes over pork chops and pour soup mixture on top. Bake at 350 degrees for 1¹/₂ hours or until pork chops are tender.

Diane Long
Delaware, OH

## QUICK & EASY VEGETABLE SALAD

*Make the night before…it's ready to eat.*

2  15¼-oz. cans petite peas, drained
2  14½-oz. cans whole green beans, drained
2  15-oz. cans shoepeg corn, drained
6  green onions, thinly sliced
4-oz. jar diced pimento
1 c. celery, chopped
1 c. sugar
1 c. white vinegar
1 c. oil
salt and pepper to taste

Combine all vegetables in a large bowl; set aside. Mix together sugar, vinegar, oil, salt and pepper; pour over vegetables and stir. Chill overnight. Serves 15 to 20.

*Rhonda Crosby*
*Bakersfield, CA*

## CELERY & ONION STUFFING

*This is so easy to make and I always get tons of compliments.*

1-lb. pkg. dry stuffing mix
10¾-oz. can cream of mushroom soup
10¾-oz. can cream of chicken soup
1 c. onion, chopped
1 c. celery, chopped

In a large mixing bowl, stir together stuffing mix, soups, one to 1½ soup cans of water, onion and celery. Place stuffing mixture into a greased 11"x7" casserole dish. Bake, covered with aluminum foil, at 325 degrees for 10 minutes. Remove foil and continue to bake for 50 minutes or until top is golden. Makes 6 servings.

*Kerry Mayer*
*Dunham Springs, LA*

**F**reeze one-inch balls of your favorite cookie dough, then thaw and bake for quick, fresh-from-the-oven treats.

# Quickie Smackeroni

a recipe from Rosalie Benson ★ Coats, NC

1 c. milk
16 oz. elbow macaroni, cooked
1 c. minced onions
¼ t. hot pepper sauce
1 lb. shredded sharp Cheddar cheese
salt & pepper to taste

In a bowl, mix ½ cup milk, macaroni, onions, hot sauce, half of cheese, salt and pepper. Spread in a 13"x9" baking dish. Cover with remaining cheese and ½ cup milk. Bake at 325 degrees, covered, for 30 minutes or until cheese is melted.

## MUSHROOMS & PEAS RICE

*My husband and I really enjoy this dish!*

8-oz. pkg. sliced mushrooms
1 T. butter
10¾-oz. can cream of mushroom soup
1 soup can milk
1¾ c. instant white rice, uncooked
1½ c. frozen peas, thawed
salt and pepper to taste

In a large skillet, sauté mushrooms in butter; set aside. In a large saucepan, bring soup and milk to a boil. Add rice to soup mixture and cover. Let cook for at least 5 minutes. When the rice is tender, stir in mushrooms, peas, salt and pepper. Makes 4 to 6 servings.

*Vickie*

## SPINACH CASSEROLE

*I like to serve this dish for Sunday dinner…it's always a hit!*

2  10-oz. pkgs frozen, chopped spinach, cooked
1-oz. pkg. dry onion soup mix
2 c. sour cream
½ c. shredded Colby Jack cheese

In a medium mixing bowl, combine spinach, soup mix and sour cream. Spoon into a greased 2-quart casserole dish; top with cheese. Bake, uncovered, at 350 degrees for 25 minutes or until heated through. Makes 8 to 10 servings.

*Carrie McNamer*
*Boston, MA*

*Cherry Coffeecake*

## CHERRY COFFEECAKE
*This is a recipe I often serve. Although this can be made ahead, it is wonderful served warm.*

18¼-oz. pkg. yellow cake mix, divided
2 eggs
²/₃ c. warm water
2 pkgs. instant dry yeast
1 c. all-purpose flour
21-oz. can cherry pie filling
5 T. margarine, melted

Mix 1½ cups cake mix with eggs, water, yeast and flour. Beat for 2 minutes. Spread into a greased 13"x9" pan. Top with pie filling. In a separate bowl, mix remaining cake mix with margarine until mixture is crumbly; sprinkle on top of pie filling. Bake at 375 degrees for 35 minutes.

Glaze:

1 c. powdered sugar
1½ T. water
1 T. corn syrup

Mix all ingredients together and drizzle over warm cake.

Gloria Kaufmann
Orrville, OH

## SPICE MUFFINS
*My favorite recipe simply because it's so easy to make!*

2 c. biscuit baking mix
½ c. milk
2 T. sugar
¼ c. applesauce
2 T. brown sugar, packed
½ t. cinnamon
½ t. nutmeg

Place all ingredients in a medium bowl. Stir together for one minute with a wooden spoon. Fill greased muffin tins ²/₃ full. Bake at 350 degrees for 15 minutes. Makes one dozen muffins.

Annette Wesgaites
Hazelton, PA

Have a christmas. time tea!

## NUTTY MAPLE PIE
*Rich and flavorful; a twist on traditional pecan pie.*

²/₃ c. sugar
6 T. unsalted butter, melted and cooled
4 eggs
1 c. maple syrup
1 c. whole hazelnuts, chopped
9-inch pie crust, unbaked

Combine sugar, butter, eggs, maple syrup and hazelnuts. Pour into pie crust and bake at 400 degrees for 10 minutes; reduce heat to 325 degrees and bake an additional 25 minutes.

Cathy Hillier
Salt Lake City, UT

## CHOCOLATE-PEANUT CANDY

*Candy made in a slow cooker...so easy!*

1 T. oil
3 T. baking cocoa
24 oz. white melting chocolate
12-oz. pkg. chocolate chips
16 oz. unsalted, dry roasted
    peanuts
16 oz. salted, dry roasted
    peanuts

Place oil, cocoa, white melting chocolate and chocolate chips in a 5-quart slow cooker. Cook over high heat until chocolate is melted and smooth. Unplug cooker and add peanuts; stir well. Drop by teaspoonfuls onto wax paper; cool. Makes about 8 dozen candies.

*Melinda Jones*
*Senath, MO*

## SPEEDY LITTLE DEVILS

*The kids just love the creamy peanut butter and marshmallow filling.*

18¼-oz. pkg. devil's food cake mix
½ c. margarine, melted
¾ c. creamy peanut butter
13-oz. jar marshmallow creme

In a large mixing bowl, thoroughly blend cake mix and margarine. Remove ½ cup cake mixture from mixing bowl and set aside for topping. Place remaining mixture in a lightly greased 13"x9" pan. Mix peanut butter and marshmallow creme together; spread onto crumb mixture. Sprinkle reserved cake mix over all. Bake at 350 degrees for 20 minutes. Makes 12 to 14 servings.

*Cathy Silvast*
*Greenfield, WI*

## PEANUT BUTTER & CHIP COOKIES

*At our house, these disappear from the cooling rack!*

2 eggs
⅓ c. water
¼ c. margarine, melted
1½ c. peanut butter
1½ c. brown sugar, packed
18¼-oz. pkg. yellow cake mix,
    divided
12-oz. pkg. chocolate chips

Beat together eggs, water, margarine, peanut butter, brown sugar and half the dry cake mix until smooth. Stir in remaining cake mix with chocolate chips. Drop by rounded teaspoonfuls onto ungreased baking sheets. Bake at 375 degrees for 10 minutes.

*Jackie Anderson*
*Deport, TX*

## RACHEL'S APRICOT MUMBLES

*The week between Christmas and New Years, we have family and in-laws, sometimes numbering 40, for dinners and breakfasts. I have many favorite recipes, but this one is so tasty and easy to prepare during the busy holiday season.*

¾ c butter, softened
1 c. brown sugar, packed
1½ c. all-purpose flour
½ t. salt
½ t. baking soda
1½ c. long-cooking oats, uncooked
16-oz. jar apricot preserves

Cream butter and sugar. Add flour, salt and baking soda; mix well. Add oats, blending thoroughly. Press half of the dough into a greased 8"x8" pan; spread preserves on top. Crumble remaining dough over preserves. Bake at 350 degrees for 25 minutes. Cool and cut into squares. Makes 16.

*Mary E. Dungan*
*Gardenville, PA*

*Rachel's Apricot Mumbles, Speedy Little Devils*

## TRIPLE FUDGE BROWNIES

*Serve them warm, right out of the oven.*

3.9-oz. pkg. instant chocolate
   pudding mix
2 c. milk
18¹/₄-oz. pkg. chocolate cake mix
12-oz. pkg. chocolate chips

Prepare pudding with milk according
to package directions. Stir in cake
mix and chocolate chips. Spread
batter in a greased 13"x9" pan.
Bake at 350 degrees for 30 to
35 minutes or until top springs
back when touched.

*Janine Edwards*
*Hulett, WY*

## 3-2-1 LEMON COOKIES

*When I first saw this recipe, I thought
that it was a joke...it sounded so odd.
Give 'em a try, they're delicious!*

3 eggs
2 18¹/₄-oz. pkgs. lemon cake mix
8-oz. container frozen whipped
   topping, thawed
1 c. powdered sugar

In a large mixing bowl, combine eggs,
cake mixes and whipped topping;
mix well. Chill dough for at least
3 hours. Drop by tablespoonfuls
into powdered sugar; coat thoroughly
and roll into balls. Place balls on
a greased baking sheet. Bake at
375 degrees for 10 to 11 minutes.
Makes 8 dozen.

*Sharon Hill*
*Roanoke, IL*

*Five-Minute Fudge, Chocolate-Butterscotch Cookies, 3-2-1 Lemon Cookies*

## CHOCOLATE-BUTTERSCOTCH COOKIES

*You can whip these up in no time. They're
perfect with a chilled glass of milk.*

1 c. corn syrup
1 c. sugar
1 c. creamy peanut butter
6 c. crispy rice cereal
1 c. semi-sweet chocolate chips
1 c. butterscotch chips

In a large saucepan, cook corn
syrup and sugar over medium heat,
stirring frequently, until mixture
comes to a boil; remove from heat.
Stir in peanut butter and cereal.
Press mixture into a greased 13"x9"
baking dish. In a double boiler, melt
chocolate and butterscotch chips,
stirring constantly, until smooth.
Spread mixture over cereal mixture.
Refrigerate for 15 minutes. Makes
48 bars.

*Michelle Lamp*
*Slayton, MN*

## FIVE-MINUTE FUDGE

*This recipe reminds me of my dad...he
always made fudge at Christmastime.*

5-oz. can evaporated milk
1²/₃ c. sugar
¹/₂ c. butter
¹/₂ t. salt
2 c. mini marshmallows
1¹/₂ c. chocolate chips
1 t. vanilla extract
¹/₂ c. chopped walnuts

Mix milk, sugar, butter and salt
together in a large saucepan over
medium-high heat. Heat to boiling,
then cook 4 minutes, stirring
constantly. Remove from heat and
add marshmallows, chocolate chips,
vanilla and walnuts. Stir for one to
2 minutes or until marshmallows
melt. Pour into a greased 8"x8"
baking pan; chill until firm. Makes
16 servings.

*Jan Prior*
*Grand Island, NE*

Fill a little red wagon with red & white lollipops, peppermints and other holiday sweets!

# Rise and SHiNE!

*Whether you need a hearty breakfast for the Christmas tree-cutting crew, a fancy brunch or a quick meal on the run, these selections will help you rise & shine on those frosty mornings!*

*Country Morning Maple Muffins, Mock Champagne Punch*

## MEL'S CHRISTMAS MORNING CASSEROLE
*A whole breakfast...baked and ready to go!*

6 eggs, slightly beaten
1/2 c. shredded Cheddar cheese
1/2 c. shredded mozzarella cheese
1 T. dried parsley
1 T. dried, minced onion
1 t. dry mustard
1 t. oregano
1 lb. ground Italian sausage, browned and drained
1 c. biscuit baking mix
2 c. milk

On Christmas Eve, mix all ingredients and pour into a lightly greased lasagna pan. Cover and refrigerate overnight. On Christmas morning, while everyone is opening gifts, pop the pan into a 350 degree oven and bake for one hour. By the time everyone is ready for breakfast, it will be hot and ready to eat. To save fat, sodium and calories, you can substitute fat-free egg substitute for eggs, low-fat baking mix for regular, use low-fat or skim milk, omit up to 1/4 cup cheese and rinse cooked Italian sausage in hot water, draining well before adding. Makes 10 to 12 servings.

Mel Wolk
St. Peters, MO

## MOCK CHAMPAGNE PUNCH
*This punch is a long-time favorite.*

1/2 c. sugar
1 c. water
6-oz. can frozen grapefruit juice concentrate
6-oz. can frozen orange juice concentrate
1/3 c. grenadine syrup
1-ltr. bottle ginger ale
Garnish: orange slices

Combine sugar and water in a saucepan; boil for 5 minutes, then cool. Add frozen juices and grenadine; refrigerate overnight. Just before serving, add ginger ale and orange slices. Makes 1 1/2 quarts.

Deborah Ocker
Harrisburg, PA

## DELIGHTFULLY CHEESY POTATOES

*My husband perfected this dish…it's a hit any time, any place! Terrific served with baked ham.*

8 to 9 potatoes
8 T. butter
8 T. all-purpose flour
1 t. salt
1/2 t. pepper
4 c. milk
8-oz. jar pasteurized process
    cheese sauce
1 1/2 c. shredded Cheddar cheese
Parmesan cheese

Cook potatoes in jackets until tender. Cool, peel and cube. Place in a large bowl. Melt butter over low heat in a heavy saucepan. Blend in flour, salt and pepper. Continue to cook over low heat until mixture is bubbly. Remove from heat and stir in milk. Return to heat and bring to a boil, stirring constantly. Boil for one minute and remove from heat. Stir in cheese sauce and one cup of Cheddar cheese; stir until cheeses melt. Transfer potatoes to a casserole dish and pour cheese mixture over potatoes; gently stir. Sprinkle generously with Parmesan and remaining Cheddar. Cover and bake at 350 degrees for one hour or until bubbly and slightly brown.

*Blanche T. Yonk*
*Petersboro, UT*

## CHRISTMAS JAM

*Spoon down the center of pancakes, then roll up and sprinkle with powdered sugar. Great on French toast or biscuits, too.*

3 c. cranberries
1 orange, peeled and seeded
10-oz. pkg. frozen, sliced
    strawberries, slightly thawed
1/4 t. ground cloves
1/4 t. ground cinnamon
4 c. sugar
1/2 c. water
1 pouch liquid fruit pectin

## Country Morning Maple Muffins

…reminiscent of a big old bowl of maple & brown sugar oatmeal!

1 1/2 c. all-purpose flour
3/4 c. long-cooking oats, uncooked
2 t. baking powder
1 t. salt
1/2 t. ground cinnamon
1/2 c. brown sugar, packed
1/4 c. margarine, softened
1 egg
1/2 c. milk
1/2 c. maple syrup
1/2 t. maple extract
1/4 c. chopped pecans

**In** a small bowl, stir together flour, oats, baking powder, salt & cinnamon. Cream together brown sugar, margarine & egg. Add milk, maple syrup & maple extract to creamed mixture until well-blended. Combine dry ingredients with creamed mixture. Stir in pecans. Spoon into greased muffin cups. Bake for 20 to 25 minutes at 350°. Serve warm.

Yields 12 muffins.

"A good, honest, wholesome hungry breakfast." -Isaac Walton

Combine cranberries and orange in a food processor; pulse until coarsely chopped. Add strawberries, cloves and cinnamon; process until mixture is finely chopped. Stir together fruit mixture, sugar and water in a large saucepan until well blended. Stirring constantly over low heat, cook for 2 minutes. Increase heat to high and bring mixture to a rolling boil; stir in liquid pectin. Stirring constantly, bring to a boil again and boil for one minute. Remove from heat; skim off foam. Ladle into hot, sterilized half-pint jars, leaving 1/4" headspace. Wipe rims and adjust lids. Process in a boiling water canner for 5 minutes. Makes 6 half-pints.

*Cora Baker*
*La Rue, OH*

*Cheese Danish Coffee Braid*

## CHEESE DANISH COFFEE BRAID

*This is a family favorite, not only because it's a tradition, but because it tastes really wonderful! It's been a part of our Christmas ritual for 21 years.*

**Pastry:**
2 pkgs. active dry yeast
½ c. warm water
6 T. sugar
1 c. butter, softened
3 eggs
1 c. sour cream
5 c. all-purpose flour, sifted

Dissolve yeast in water, then add sugar. Cream together butter, eggs and sour cream. Alternating each, add flour and yeast mixture to the sour cream mixture; combine thoroughly. Cover and let rise in a warm place about 1 hour or until double in bulk. Divide dough into 4 sections for braiding. Roll each section into a 12"x9" rectangle and place on a greased baking sheet.

**Cheese Filling:**
3  8-oz. pkgs. cream cheese, softened
3 egg yolks
8 T. sugar
3 t. vanilla extract

Combine all ingredients and beat well with mixer. Spoon the filling into the center of each rectangle of dough and, using scissors or a sharp knife, cut the dough from the outside edge toward the filling into one-inch strips. Alternating one strip from each side, fold the strips at a criss-cross angle across the filling so it resembles a braid. Cover with a cloth and let rise in a warm place for about an hour. Bake at 350 degrees for 20 to 25 minutes. Drizzle with glaze. Makes 4 braids.

**Glaze:**
4 c. powdered sugar
⅓ c. orange juice
1 t. lemon juice

*Leigh Ann Ramey*
*Huber Heights, OH*

# EARLY A.M. French T·O·A·S·T
## — a make-ahead dish —
◆ ◆ ◆ ◆ ◆ ◆ ◆

1 c. BROWN SUGAR, PACKED
½ c. BUTTER
2 T. CORN SYRUP
5 EGGS
1½ c. MILK
1 t. VANILLA EXTRACT
1 LOAF FRENCH BREAD, CUT INTO THICK SLICES

In a medium saucepan over medium heat, mix & melt brown sugar, butter & corn syrup. Spray a baking dish with non-stick vegetable oil and fill with the butter mixture.

Mix eggs, milk & vanilla. Arrange bread slices in baking dish. Pour egg mixture over bread; don't miss any area ᵥ use all the mixture. Any extra will be soaked up by the bread.

Cover dish and refrigerate overnight. The next morning, simply uncover and slip into a 350° oven for 30 minutes, then serve.

WHO KNEW I COULD BE SO QUICK & DELICIOUS?

*Warm Country Gingerbread Waffles, Colorado Cocoa*

## COUNTRY SCRAMBLE

*All of our family's favorite breakfast foods in one casserole!*

2 c. frozen hash browns
1 c. fully cooked ham, chopped
1/2 c. onion, chopped
6 eggs, beaten
salt and pepper to taste
1 c. shredded Cheddar cheese
Garnish: fresh chives, minced

In a large skillet, sauté hash browns, ham and onion for 10 minutes or until hash browns are tender. In a small bowl, combine eggs, salt and pepper. Add to hash brown mixture and cook, stirring occasionally, until eggs are set. Remove from heat and gently stir in cheese. Spoon onto serving platter; sprinkle with chives.

*Dorothy Foor*
*Jeromesville, OH*

## WARM COUNTRY GINGERBREAD WAFFLES

*Can be served with brown sugar, powdered sugar, hot maple syrup or berries.*

2 c. all-purpose flour
1 t. ground cinnamon
1/2 t. ground ginger
1/2 t. salt
1 c. molasses
1/2 c. butter
1 1/2 t. baking soda
1 c. buttermilk
1 egg

Combine flour, cinnamon, ginger and salt. Heat molasses and butter until butter melts. Remove from heat and stir in baking soda. Add buttermilk and egg, then add flour mixture. Cook in a preheated, oiled waffle iron until golden. Makes 12 four-inch waffles.

## FRUIT SALAD WITH ORANGE DRESSING

*Add any fruits in season to this special creamy dressing.*

2 6.1-oz. cans mandarin oranges, drained
2 15 1/4-oz. cans sliced peaches, drained
2 20-oz. cans pineapple tidbits, drained
1 apple with peel, cored and diced
3/4 c. sour cream
3-oz. box instant vanilla pudding mix
1 1/2 c. milk
6-oz. can frozen orange juice concentrate, thawed

Mix all fruits together in a large bowl. Whisk together sour cream, pudding mix and milk; stir in orange juice concentrate. Pour over fruit and refrigerate overnight.

*Shirll Kosmal*
*Delaware, OH*

## COLORADO COCOA

*Serve in jumbo mugs with whipped cream and a dash of cinnamon!*

3 T. baking cocoa
2 T. sugar
4 c. milk
1 oz. semi-sweet chocolate, shaved

In a saucepan, mix together cocoa and sugar, then pour in cold milk. Stir until sugar is well blended; add shaved chocolate. Stirring constantly with a wooden spoon, heat until milk is almost at the boiling point and chocolate is melted. Do not let milk boil.

*Pat Akers*
*Stanton, CA*

*"I never had a piece of toast Particularly long and wide, But fell upon the sanded floor, And always on the buttered side."*

*— James Payne*

**109**

*Sunrise Ham*

## WAKE-UP SCONES
*With coffee, tea or even cocoa...you'll love 'em!*

1³/₄ c. all-purpose flour
1/₃ c. gingersnap cookies, crushed
1/₄ c. sugar
1¹/₂ t. baking powder
1/₂ t. baking soda
1/₄ t. salt
1/₄ c. cold butter, sliced
1/₂ c. buttermilk
1 egg, beaten
10 walnut halves

Combine first 6 ingredients; cut in butter until mixture resembles coarse crumbs. Add buttermilk and egg; stir until just moistened. Turn dough onto a lightly floured surface; knead lightly 4 times. Pat dough into a 10-inch circle on a lightly greased baking sheet; score into 10 wedges. Bake at 400 degrees for 15 minutes or until golden. Drizzle scones with espresso glaze; cut into 10 wedges and top each with a walnut half. Makes 10 servings.

Espresso Glaze:
1 T. hot water
2 t. instant coffee granules
1 c. powdered sugar

Combine hot water and coffee granules in a small mixing bowl; stir until coffee dissolves. Add powdered sugar; mix until smooth.
*Laura Fuller*
*Ft. Wayne, IN*

Not all biscuits have to be round...use cookie cutters to create fun whimsical shapes like snowmen, stars or snowflakes.

Transform ordinary orange juice into sunrise punch! Freeze cranberry juice cocktail into ice cubes, then fill your juice pitcher and glasses with cranberry cubes before pouring in the orange juice.

## SUNRISE HAM
*Fresh fruit is a refreshing complement to this creamy dish.*

1 c. cooked ham, diced
1 c. sliced mushrooms
1 T. margarine, melted
4 eggs
1 c. sour cream
1 c. cottage cheese
1/₂ c. grated Parmesan cheese
1/₄ c. all-purpose flour
1/₂ t. dill weed
1/₂ t. dry mustard
1/₈ t. nutmeg
1/₈ t. pepper
1 c. shredded Swiss cheese
1/₂ c. fresh parsley, chopped

Cook ham in a skillet until lightly browned; set aside. Sauté mushrooms in margarine until tender; mix with ham and place in a greased 9" deep-dish pie plate. Combine eggs, sour cream, cottage cheese, Parmesan cheese, flour, dill weed, mustard, nutmeg and pepper in a blender; blend until smooth. Sprinkle Swiss cheese and parsley over ham and mushrooms. Pour egg mixture into pie plate. Bake at 350 degrees for 45 minutes or until set; let stand 10 minutes before cutting. Makes 6 to 8 servings.

*Kristi Stahl*
*Hutchinson, MN*

## HOLIDAY QUICHE

*Double the recipe! Freeze the second quiche and you have a quick meal when time is short!*

10-oz. pkg. frozen chopped
    spinach
2 c. shredded sharp Cheddar
    cheese
2 T. all-purpose flour
1 c. milk
2 eggs, beaten
3 slices bacon, cooked, drained
    and crumbled
1/8 t. pepper
9" pie shell
Garnish: tomato wedges and
    fresh parsley

Cook the spinach; drain and cool. In a bowl, toss the cheese with the flour. Add spinach and remaining ingredients; mix well. Pour into the pie shell and bake at 350 degrees for one hour. Cool for 10 minutes and slice into pieces. Garnish each slice with a wedge of tomato and parsley. Serves 6.

*Wendy Lee Paffenroth*
*Pine Island, NY*

## ESCALLOPED APPLES

*An old-fashioned dish that goes great with any meal!*

1/2 c. butter
2 c. fresh bread crumbs
4 tart apples, cored, peeled and
    sliced
1/2 c. sugar
1/4 t. ground cinnamon
1/4 t. ground cloves

Melt butter in a saucepan. Add bread crumbs and toast lightly for about 2 minutes; set aside. Toss apples with sugar, cinnamon and cloves. In an oiled 8"x8" baking dish, layer half of the apples and half of the toasted bread crumbs. Repeat with the remaining apples and bread crumbs. Bake at 325 degrees, covered, for 45 minutes or until apples are tender.

*Jennifer Heinl*
*Pittsburgh, PA*

## SAVORY BRUNCH BREAD

*Delicious with your favorite omelet and freshly squeezed orange juice.*

1/4 c. grated Parmesan cheese
3 T. sesame seeds
1/2 t. dried basil, crushed
1 pkg. 24 unbaked frozen yeast
    rolls
1/4 c. butter or margarine, melted
2 t. real bacon bits

Grease a 10-inch fluted tube pan. In small bowl, combine Parmesan cheese, sesame seeds and basil. Add 1/3 of mix to pan and turn to coat sides. Place 10 frozen rolls in pan and drizzle with half of the butter. Sprinkle with half of the remaining cheese mix and bacon bits. Add remaining rolls. Drizzle with remaining butter and sprinkle with remaining cheese. Cover; let rolls thaw and rise overnight (12 to 24 hours) in the refrigerator. The next day, let stand at room temperature 30 minutes. Bake uncovered at 350 degrees for 20 minutes. Cover with foil and bake 10 to 15 minutes more or until golden brown. Remove from pan to wire rack; serve warm. Serves 12.

## CHILLED VANILLA COFFEE

*For a special treat, serve in frosty holiday glasses.*

2 T. instant coffee granules
3/4 c. warm water
14-oz. can sweetened condensed
    milk
1 t. vanilla extract
4 c. ice cubes

Dissolve coffee in water; blend in condensed milk and vanilla. Pour mixture into a blender and gradually add ice cubes; blend until smooth. Serve immediately. Makes 4 servings.

*Cori Ritter*
*Port Washington, WI*

## OtHer Breakfast GooDiES:

★ dress up a naked grapefruit half with a drizzle of honey & a dash of cinnamon & a quick sit under the broiler for 2 minutes!

★ frozen fruit salads in muffin tins are delicious breakfast treats served alongside waffles.

★ puree ripe fruit & add softened butter & powdered sugar to it to make delightful homemade fruit butters for pancakes & muffins!

*Add flair to the breakfast table with gourmet butters! They're easy to make: Just soften a stick of butter and mix it with your choice of flavorings...try grated orange peel and mint, ground hazelnuts and cinnamon or lemon zest and poppy seed...experiment to make your own combinations. Roll mixture into a log, wrap in wax paper and chill.*

*Grab your apron, plug in the mixer and preheat the oven…it's time to open the doors of the Christmas Bakery! This hand-picked collection features the very best cookies, pies, cakes and sweet breads to delight your family & friends.*

*Caramel Rolls, Julekage*

## CARAMEL ROLLS

*Growing up in a small village in Wisconsin, Grandma would send us to a nearby cheese factory for fresh cream and butter for these rolls.*

1 c. light brown sugar, packed
$\frac{1}{2}$ c. whipping cream
3$\frac{1}{2}$ to 4 c. all-purpose flour, divided
$\frac{3}{4}$ c. sugar, divided
$\frac{1}{2}$ t. salt
1 pkg. active dry yeast
1 c. water
$\frac{1}{2}$ c. plus 2 T. butter, divided
1 egg, beaten
2 t. cinnamon

Combine brown sugar and whipping cream in a saucepan; cook over medium heat until sugar is dissolved. Pour into an ungreased 13"x9" pan and set aside. In a large bowl, combine 1$\frac{1}{2}$ cups flour, $\frac{1}{4}$ cup sugar, salt and yeast; blend. In a small saucepan, heat water and 2 tablespoons butter until very warm. Add warm liquid and egg to flour mixture. Blend at low speed of an electric mixer for 3 minutes. By hand, stir in remaining flour to form a stiff dough. On a floured surface, knead 2 to 3 minutes. Press or roll dough to form a 15"x7" rectangle. In a small bowl, combine cinnamon, remaining $\frac{1}{2}$ cup sugar and $\frac{1}{2}$ cup butter; spread over dough. Starting at a long side, roll up tightly; seal edges. Cut into 15 rolls. Place rolls, cut side down, on top of brown sugar mixture. Cover and let rise in a warm place until light and double in size, 35 to 45 minutes. Bake at 400 degrees for 20 to 23 minutes or until lightly golden.

Lisa Colombo
Appleton, WI

# JULEKAGE

*A traditional Norwegian sweet bread.*

1½ c. raisins
³/₄ c. candied fruit, diced
½ c. brandy or orange juice
6 to 7 c. all-purpose flour, divided
4 pkgs. active dry yeast
³/₄ c. lukewarm water
²/₃ c. plus 2 T. sugar, divided
½ c. milk
1 c. unsalted butter
1 t. salt
2 t. cardamom
zest of one orange and one lemon
1 egg yolk, beaten
1 T. water
Garnish: sugar and blanched
    almond halves

Combine raisins, candied fruit and brandy; let stand one hour. Drain, reserving fruit and brandy. Toss fruit with enough flour to lightly coat. Sprinkle yeast in lukewarm water, add 2 tablespoons sugar and set aside. Combine milk, butter, salt and ²/₃ cup sugar over medium heat. When butter has melted, remove from heat and stir in 2 teaspoons reserved brandy, cardamom and zest. Cool to lukewarm and combine with yeast mixture. Gradually add 5 cups of flour. Turn onto a floured board and knead for 10 minutes, adding more flour, if needed. Place dough in a lightly floured bowl. Dust top of dough with flour, cover and let rise about 45 minutes or until double in bulk and no longer springy when pressed with your fingertips. Punch dough down and divide in half. Shape each portion into a loaf; place loaves in 8"x4" loaf pans. Combine egg yolk and water; brush over tops of bread. Sprinkle with sugar and blanched almonds. Let rise again until double in bulk. Bake at 350 degrees for one hour or until golden. Drizzle with your favorite powdered sugar icing, if desired.

*Juanita Williams*
*Jacksonville, OR*

*Chocolate-Praline Cake*

# CHOCOLATE-PRALINE CAKE

*Each year, it's a tradition of ours to make a special chocolate cake.*

Cake:
3  1-oz. sqs. semisweet chocolate,
    finely chopped
5 T. unsalted butter
⅓ c. vegetable oil
²/₃ c. water
⅓ c. baking cocoa
1 c. plus 2 T. sugar
1 egg, beaten
1¼ c. all-purpose flour
2 t. baking powder
⅓ c. buttermilk

Combine first 4 ingredients in a small saucepan over medium heat. Stir constantly until smooth; remove from heat. Combine baking cocoa and sugar; whisk into chocolate mixture until well blended. Transfer to a large bowl; cool. Add egg; set aside. Sift flour and baking powder together; add to chocolate mixture, mixing well. Stir in buttermilk. Line a 9" round cake pan with parchment paper. Butter paper and dust with flour, removing any excess. Add batter; bake at 350 degrees for 30 to 35 minutes. Cool 5 minutes; invert on a wire rack to finish cooling.

Frosting:
2 T. butter, softened
8 oz. mascarpone cheese
2 t. vanilla extract
4³/₄ c. sifted powdered sugar
1 to 2 T. milk

Beat together butter and mascarpone cheese with an electric mixer; add vanilla. Add powdered sugar, beating until combined. Add milk to frosting until desired spreading consistency.

Praline:
³/₄ c. sugar
¼ c. water
½ c. whole almonds, chopped and
    toasted
½ c. hazelnuts, chopped and
    toasted

Combine sugar and water in a saucepan. Whisking constantly, bring to a boil over medium-high heat until mixture becomes light golden brown. Remove from heat; stir in nuts. Pour on a greased foil-lined baking sheet. Cool, then crush with a rolling pin. Sprinkle over cake. Makes 10 to 12 servings.

*Erica Wieschenberg*
*Towaco, NJ*

## MORAVIAN SUGAR COOKIES

*The secret to these cookies is the buttermilk. Double or triple this one; they freeze really well!*

1/2 c. margarine, softened
1/2 c. shortening
1 c. sugar
1 c. brown sugar, packed
2 eggs
1 t. vanilla extract
1/8 t. salt
1/2 t. baking soda
2 T. buttermilk
4 c. all-purpose flour

Cream margarine and shortening with sugars. Add eggs, vanilla, and salt; mix well. In a small cup, add baking soda to buttermilk. Let sit one minute, then add to the sugar mixture. Add the flour and mix well. Divide dough in half and chill up to 2 hours. On a floured surface, roll out dough to 1/8-inch thickness and use 2-inch Christmas-shaped cookie cutters to cut dough. Bake at 375 degrees for 5 to 7 minutes or until firm. (Do not overbake or expect them to turn brown). They will melt in your mouth! Makes 5 dozen.

## APRICOT BARS

*These cookies refrigerate well.*

3/4 c. butter, softened
1 c. sugar
1/2 t. vanilla extract
1 egg
1/2 t. salt
2 c. all-purpose flour
1 1/2 c. coconut
12-oz. jar apricot preserves
1/2 c. pecans, chopped

Cream butter and sugar. Add vanilla, egg, salt, flour and coconut; mix well. Spread 3/4 of the mixture in a greased 11"x7" oven-proof glass dish. Spread preserves on top. Combine the remaining dough and nuts; crumble over preserves. Bake at 350 degrees for 40 to 45 minutes, until golden. Cut into bars while still warm. Makes 1 dozen.

*Lesa Lafferty*
*Indiahoma, OK*

## TOASTED HAZELNUT COOKIES

*Oh...the warm, toasty flavor of hazelnuts!*

3 c. all-purpose flour
2 t. baking powder
1/2 t. salt
11-oz. jar chocolate-hazelnut spread*
1/4 c. shortening
1 1/3 c. sugar
1 t. vanilla extract
2 eggs
1/3 c. milk
1/2 c. hazelnuts, chopped and toasted
1 to 2 c. hazelnuts, finely chopped
3/4 c. powdered sugar, sifted

Stir together flour, baking powder and salt. In a separate bowl, combine chocolate-hazelnut spread and shortening; beat with electric mixer on medium speed until combined. Add sugar and beat until fluffy. Add vanilla and eggs; beat until combined. Gradually add flour mixture and milk, alternating until combined. Stir in 1/2 c. chopped hazelnuts. Cover and chill 2 to 3 hours, until firm. Shape dough into 1 1/2-inch balls. Roll balls in finely chopped hazelnuts, then in powdered sugar. Place 2 inches apart on a lightly greased baking sheet. Bake at 375 degrees for 8 to 10 minutes or until surface is cracked. Cool on a rack. Makes 5 to 6 dozen.

*Note: Chocolate-flavored hazelnut spread can be found in many groceries and gourmet food shops.

*It's oh-so easy to make your own vanilla sugar for flavoring cookies, pastries or even a cup of coffee! Simply put a vanilla bean in a jar of sugar and seal tightly...the longer it sits, the stronger the flavor.*

## ★ Snicker Doodles ★
### ...everybody loves 'em!

1 1/2 c. sugar
1/2 c. margarine, softened
1 t. vanilla extract
2 eggs
2 c. all-purpose flour
1 t. cream of tartar
1/2 t. baking soda
1/4 t. salt
2 T. sugar & 2 t. cinnamon

Beat together sugar & margarine in large bowl until light & fluffy. Add vanilla & eggs ~ mix 'til well blended. Stir in flour, cream of tartar, soda & salt. Mix well ~ set aside. Combine sugar & cinnamon in small bowl. Shape dough into 1" balls ~ roll in cinnamon-sugar mixture. Place on ungreased baking sheet 2" apart. Bake at 350° for 10 to 14 minutes. Remove immediately to cool on wire racks. Makes 3 to 4 dozen cookies.

## GRANDMA MILLER'S NUTMEG LOGS

*You'll want more than just one!*

**Cookies:**
1 c. butter, softened
3/4 c. sugar
1 egg, slightly beaten
2 t. vanilla extract
2 t. rum extract
1 t. nutmeg
3 c. all-purpose flour

Preheat oven to 350 degrees. Cream together butter and sugar; add egg. Stir in vanilla and rum extract. Add nutmeg and flour to creamed ingredients. Divide dough into a workable size. Roll into long strips and cut into 1½-inch lengths. Place on ungreased baking sheet. (Since cookies don't spread, they can be placed close together.) Bake for 10 to 15 minutes.

**Frosting:**
3 T. butter, softened
1/2 t. vanilla extract
1 t. rum extract
2½ c. powdered sugar
3 T. milk
1/4 t. nutmeg

Mix first 4 ingredients together; add milk until desired consistency. After cookies have cooled, frost each, then run the tines of a fork across frosting to resemble a log. Sprinkle with nutmeg.

*Jenny Miller*
*Hollywood, FL*

We all know that spices add wonderful flavor to our holiday baking, but where do they come from? Well, cloves are actually flower buds, and cinnamon is the bark of a tree. Allspice is a berry, and nutmeg is a fruit pit!

To make an elegant party dessert, quickly roll scoops of ice cream in shredded coconut, then serve on chilled plates with chocolate sauce on the side. Experiment with different flavors of ice cream and add chopped nuts or colorful candy sprinkles to the coconut.

*Clockwise from left: Moravian Sugar Cookies, Snickerdoodles, Apricot Bars, Toasted Hazelnut Cookies, Grandma Miller's Nutmeg Logs*

Have a spot of tea and maybe two or three

# Cheery Cherry Chocolate Dots

a favorite recipe from SUSAN EDWARDS ★ GLENOLDEN, PA

1 c. powdered sugar
1 c. butter, softened
2 t. maraschino cherry liquid
½ t. almond extract
4 drops red food coloring
2·¼ c. all-purpose flour

½ t. salt
½ c. maraschino cherries, chopped & drained, liquid reserved
48 milk chocolate drops

○ ○ ★ ○ ○

Combine powdered sugar, butter, cherry liquid, almond extract and food coloring; blend well. Add in flour and salt; mix well. Stir in cherries and shape dough into one-inch balls. Place 2 inches apart on ungreased baking sheets; bake at 350 degrees for 8 to 10 minutes. Remove from oven and immediately top each cookie with a chocolate drop, pressing down firmly. Makes 48.

## ULTIMATE CHOCOLATE BROWNIES

*A brownie-lover's delight! You can't eat just one...they are heavenly.*

¾ c. baking cocoa
½ t. baking soda
⅔ c. butter, melted and divided
½ c. boiling water
2 c. sugar
2 eggs
1⅓ c. all-purpose flour
1 t. vanilla extract
¼ t. salt

½ c. chopped pecans
11½-oz. pkg. semi-sweet chocolate chunks

In a large bowl, combine cocoa and baking soda; blend in ⅓ cup of melted butter. Add boiling water and stir until well blended. Mix in sugar, eggs and remaining butter; blend in flour, vanilla and salt. Stir in pecans and chocolate chunks. Pour into a greased 13"x9" pan and bake at 350 degrees for 35 to 40 minutes. Makes 3 dozen.

Aileen Leaton
Bethlehem, PA

## FROSTED BUTTERSCOTCH COOKIES

*Get out your favorite cookie cutters for these decorated delights!*

Cookies:
1 c. butterscotch chips
1 c. butter, softened
½ c. brown sugar, packed
½ c. sugar
½ t. salt
1 egg
2 T. milk
2 t. vanilla extract
3 c. all-purpose flour

Melt butterscotch chips in a small saucepan over low heat, stirring constantly. Pour into large mixing bowl; add butter, sugars, salt, egg, milk and vanilla. Add flour; beat at low speed until mixed well. Divide dough in half and wrap in plastic wrap. Refrigerate one hour. Roll out dough on lightly floured surface to ⅛-inch thickness. Cut into your favorite shapes. Place one inch apart on lightly greased baking sheets. Bake at 350 degrees for 5 to 8 minutes or until edges are golden. Allow to cool before frosting. Makes about 4 dozen.

Frosting:
2 c. powdered sugar
¼ c. butter, softened
2 T. milk
1 t. vanilla extract
food coloring

Combine all frosting ingredients and beat at low speed until fluffy. Spoon frosting into a pastry bag fitted with a small round tip. Pipe frosting onto cookies.

*It's an old English custom to wrap tiny treasures in paper and bake them inside the Christmas cake. A bell means a wedding soon, a thimble blesses its owner, a wishbone grants any wish and a horseshoe means good luck. Be sure to let your guests know about the surprises before they dig in!*

## THREE SISTERS' APPLE & ORANGE CAKE

*I can remember this cake as a child and the aroma that filled the house. Named for my mother and her two sisters, one taste takes me back to my childhood.*

Cake:
1 c. shortening
2 c. sugar
4 eggs
3 c. all-purpose flour
1/2 t. baking soda
1/2 t. salt
1 c. buttermilk
1 t. vanilla extract

Combine shortening and sugar; add eggs, one at a time, mixing well after each addition. In a separate bowl, sift flour, baking soda and salt together. Add to sugar mixture, alternating with buttermilk, beginning and ending with flour mixture. Mix just until blended; stir in vanilla. Divide between 2 greased and floured 9" round baking pans; bake at 350 degrees for 30 to 35 minutes. Cool 5 minutes; remove from pans, then frost.

Frosting:
6 apples
3 oranges
1 1/2 c. sugar
1/2 t. vanilla extract

Core and grate one apple with peel intact; set aside. Peel, core and grate remaining 5 apples. With peel intact and seeds removed, grate 2 oranges. Peel, grate and seed second orange. In a large saucepan, toss together all the grated apples and oranges with remaining ingredients and cook over medium heat about 45 minutes or until thickened, stirring constantly. Spread one cup warm frosting between cooled cake layers; spread remaining frosting on top and sides of cake. Makes 12 servings.

*Marsha McKoy*
*Rome, GA*

## POPPY SEED BREAD

*An old-fashioned sweet bread.*

3 eggs
1 1/2 c. milk
1 1/8 c. vegetable oil
1 1/2 t. vanilla extract
1 1/2 t. almond extract
1 1/2 t. butter flavoring
3 c. all-purpose flour
2 1/3 c. sugar
2 T. poppy seed
1 1/2 t. salt
1/2 t. baking powder

Beat eggs together in a large mixing bowl. Add all liquid ingredients and mix well; add dry ingredients. Pour into 2 lightly greased loaf pans. Bake at 325 degrees for one hour. Let cool in pans for 10 minutes.

Glaze:
1/4 c. orange juice
1/2 c. sugar
1/2 t. vanilla extract
1/2 t. almond extract
1/2 t. butter flavoring

Mix all ingredients together until sugar is dissolved completely. Pour glaze over bread in pans; cool completely.

*Linda Thomas*
*Everett, WA*

*Three Sisters' Apple & Orange Cake*

117

*Orange Biscuits*

*Mix up this quick & tasty treat for drop-in company!*

2 eggs
1 c. sugar
1 c. dairy eggnog
1/2 c. margarine, melted
2 t. rum extract
1 t. vanilla extract
2 1/4 c. all-purpose flour
2 t. baking powder
1/4 t. nutmeg

Beat eggs in a large bowl, then add next 5 ingredients, blending well. Add remaining ingredients and stir until just moist. Pour into a greased loaf pan and bake at 350 degrees for 45 to 50 minutes.

*Kathy Bolyea*
*Naples, FL*

## ORANGE BISCUITS

*My grandmother kept a journal and always included lots of recipes alongside her memories. I remember her always serving these with ham...oh, the aroma from the kitchen was wonderful!*

1/2 c. orange juice
3/4 c. sugar, divided
1/4 c. butter
2 t. orange zest
2 c. all-purpose flour
1 T. baking powder
1/2 t. salt
1/4 c. shortening
3/4 c. milk
1/4 c. butter, softened
1/2 t. cinnamon

Combine orange juice, 1/2 cup sugar, butter and orange zest in a medium saucepan. Cook and stir over medium heat for 2 minutes. Fill 12 ungreased muffin tins each with 1 tablespoon of mixture; set aside. Sift together flour, baking powder and salt; cut in shortening until mixture resembles coarse crumbs. Stir in milk and mix with a fork until mixture forms a ball. On a lightly floured surface, knead dough for one minute. Roll into a 9-inch square about 1/2-inch thick; spread with softened butter. Combine cinnamon and remaining 1/4 c. sugar; sprinkle over dough. Roll up dough and cut into 12 slices about 3/4-inch thick. Place slices, cut side down, in muffin cups. Bake at 450 degrees for 14 to 17 minutes. Cool for 2 to 3 minutes; remove from pan. Makes one dozen.

*Peg Baker*
*La Rue, OH*

## Holly's CHOCOLATE SILK PIE

...the RICH FILLING IS AS SMOOTH AS SILK!

3/4 c. BROWN SUGAR, PACKED
1/4 c. MARGARINE OR BUTTER, SOFTENED
3 EGGS
1·1/4 c. SEMI-SWEET CHOCOLATE CHIPS, MELTED
1·1/2 t. INSTANT COFFEE GRANULES
1 t. ALMOND EXTRACT
1 c. ALMONDS, TOASTED & CHOPPED
1/4 c. ALL-PURPOSE FLOUR
1 UNBAKED PASTRY SHELL
1/2 c. WHOLE ALMONDS

In a mixing bowl, beat brown sugar & margarine until fluffy. Beat in one egg at a time. Mix in chocolate, coffee & almond extract. Add chopped nuts & flour—mix well. Pour filling into unbaked pie shell. Decorate top with whole almonds. Bake on lower rack in oven at 375 degrees. Cool. Chill at least one hour before serving.

*Raspberry Crunch Cheesecake*

## RASPBERRY CRUNCH CHEESECAKE

*Make this the night before; a great time-saver!*

1½ c. quick-cooking oats, uncooked
1½ c. brown sugar, packed
1½ c. all-purpose flour
1 c. butter
¾ c. nuts, chopped
5  8-oz. pkgs. cream cheese
1 c. sugar
¼ c. cornstarch
½ c. whipping cream
4 eggs
10-oz. jar seedless raspberry jam

In a bowl, mix together oats, brown sugar and flour. Cut in the butter to make crumbs; add nuts. Press 5½ cups of mixture into the bottom and halfway up the sides of a greased 10" springform pan. Save the remaining ¾ cup crumbs for the top of cake. Bake at 350 degrees for 15 to 18 minutes to set crust. In a large bowl, with an electric mixer, beat cream cheese, sugar, cornstarch and cream. Add eggs, one at a time, beating well after each addition. Pour into crust. Heat jam in microwave 30 seconds. Spoon jam over batter and swirl into batter.

Bake at 325 degrees for 1 hour and 15 minutes. Top hot cake with reserved crumbs. Return to oven and bake for 15 to 20 minutes or until crust is a golden brown. Turn off oven and let cake sit in the oven for one hour. Chill overnight.

Debi Timperley
Stanton, NE

119

# INSTRUCTIONS

## FLIP PHOTO CALENDAR
(shown on page 10)

Keep up with your family's growth (and adventures!) during the year with this quick & easy photo calendar. Use decorative-edge craft scissors to cut a background from fabric, then glue it to the front of a 5½"x8½" spiral-bound journal. Glue an inventory tag on the fabric for a label, then glue a charm or 2 around the label. Cut shapes from decorative paper and glue to the pages…glue photographs and small inventory tags to write comments on to the paper shapes.

## FRAME GARLAND
(shown on pages 12 and 13)

Craft this simple garland to display a few of your favorite photos this holiday season. It can be hung anywhere…or, just hang the frames everywhere!

Purchase paper maché frames in assorted sizes…use decorative ribbons, rick-rack, lace, buttons, charms, artificial holly leaves or tiny bells to adorn the frames. Use rubber stamps or stickers to add accents where needed. On some of the frames, you may want to glue on a tiny paper bag or envelope to hold a decorated tag containing written memories about the photograph. When you're through embellishing the frames, mount a photograph in each frame, then use clothespins to hang them on a length of jute…twist small sprigs of greenery onto the jute between the frames.

## NAMETAG ORNAMENTS
(shown on pages 14 and 15)

For each nametag ornament, cut a dog-ear-shaped tag from white card stock; use a craft glue stick to glue the tag to a Christmasy color of card stock, then trim the card stock ¼" larger on each side than the tag. Stamp a name on the tag, then attach a fabric or sticker border around the name. Use a fine-point marker to write messages along the tag edges. Punch a hole at the top of the tag and apply a hole reinforcement. Use bright red ribbon to attach the ornaments to a **Nametag Family Tree**.

## NAMETAG FAMILY TREE
(shown on page 15)

For the tree trunk, cut a ½" diameter dowel to 27" long. Cut 6", 8½" and 15" long branches from a ⅜" diameter dowel; drill a tiny hole through the center of each branch. Prime, then paint the pieces green; allow to dry. Allowing room for the trunk to be "planted" in a pot, nail the branches on the trunk. Crisscross, then tie, red raffia around each branch at the trunk to cover the nail. Glue one red wooden bead to the end of each branch; glue a red wooden finial to the top of the tree. Place the tree trunk in a red flowerpot or can filled with sand or gravel; cover the top of the container with holly and berries.

## FLANNEL STOCKINGS
(shown on pages 16 and 17)

Tired of the same old stockings? This year, why not adorn your chimney with these quick & easy stockings that even Santa is sure to admire!

*Refer to Embroidery Stitches, page 132, for some "stitching how-to's" from your Country Friends®.*

### Basic Stocking

**1.** Referring to *Making Patterns*, page 131, and using the patterns on pages 133 and 134, draw an entire stocking pattern on the dull side of freezer paper. Use a warm iron to press the paper, shiny side down, onto a folded piece of felt large enough to accommodate the pattern (this keeps the felt from stretching out of shape); pin the pattern in place and use pinking shears to cut out 2 stocking shapes.

**2.** Decide which heel pattern you want to use, then trace it and the toe pattern onto the paper side of fusible web. Fuse the web to desired fabric, flannel or felt, then use pinking shears to cut out the shape. Arrange the heel and toe pieces on the stocking front and fuse in place; use pinking shears to trim the edges even with the stocking. Use 3 strands of embroidery floss to work *Blanket Stitches* along the inside heel and toe edges.

**3.** Don't sew the stocking pieces together yet…that will come after embellishing the stocking front.

### Button Flower Stocking
Select assorted sizes of red buttons for "flowers"; cut round pieces of green

felt a little larger than some of the buttons. Referring to the photograph as a placement guide, use green floss to sew flowers onto the stocking front…remember to add the green circles under a few buttons. Use 6 strands of green embroidery floss to work *Running Stitches* for stems and branches to join the flowers together.

### Pocket Stocking
Trace the pocket pattern from page 134 onto tracing paper. Fuse the wrong sides of 2 pieces of coordinating fabrics, large enough to accommodate the pocket pattern, together; use the pattern to cut a pocket from the fused fabrics. Pin the pocket on the stocking front; use floss to sew sides and bottom to stocking. Fold pocket point down and sew a button at the tip to secure in place.

### Tree Stocking
Trace the tree and trunk patterns from page 134 onto the paper side of fusible web. Fuse web pieces to 2 shades of green felt, then cut out tree and trunk. Arrange tree and trunk on stocking front and fuse in place. Work *Blanket Stitches* around the tree. Use embroidery floss to sew assorted red buttons to the tree, then top it off with a red star-shaped button sewn to the point.

### Finishing the Stocking
**4.** Now, place the stocking front and back together (right sides out) and use 6 strands of embroidery floss to work *Blanket Stitches* along the edges to sew the pieces together.

**5.** For a cuff, cut a 4"x11" piece from desired trim fabric. (If you're going to fringe the cuff, cut it 4½" wide.) Matching right sides together, sew the short ends together. Matching the seam in the cuff with the heel-side seam in the stocking and matching top edges, place cuff, right-side out, inside stocking, then sew pieces together ¼" from the top. Turn cuff to the outside of the stocking.

**6.** To finish the cuff, either fringe the outside edge or press it ¼" to the wrong side and attach jumbo rick-rack along the inside edge, leaving half of the width of the rick-rack extending past the edge.

**7.** For a hanger, sew the ends of a 10" length of grosgrain ribbon together inside the stocking at the heel seam.

## SNOWMAN DRAFT STOPPER

(continued from page 26)

**3.** For each leg, match right sides and sew fabric pieces together along the long edge. Leaving top edge open, sew 2 boot pieces together. Turn the leg and boot right-side out. Place 1 tablespoon of uncooked rice in heel of boot, then stuff with fiberfill to about 1/2" below the top. Place 1/2" of one end of the leg in the boot; work *Running Stitches* along the top edge of the boot to secure leg in place; stuff leg with fiberfill. Use embroidery floss to sew "laces" on boot.

**4.** Leaving the top open, sew 2 arm pieces together for each arm, turn right-side out and add 1 tablespoon of uncooked rice.

**5.** With arms and legs angled to the inside, pin arms and legs to the right side of the front body piece where indicated on the pattern; baste in place. Matching edges and right sides, pin the body pieces together. Leaving a 4" opening at head, sew the body pieces together; turn snowman right side out. Fill the bottom of the body with rice, then stuff with fiberfill and sew opening closed.

**6.** Fold the hat piece in half. Referring to **Fig. 1**, mark the hat piece diagonally. Sew along the marks and trim the seam allowances to 1/4"; do not turn hat right-side out. For the tassel, cutting to within 3/4" of one long edge, make clips 1/4" apart on tassel piece. Roll the tassel tightly and glue to secure. Place the solid edge of the tassel inside the end of the hat; wrap floss several times around the end of the hat and tie tightly. Sew short ends of cuff together. Matching wrong sides and raw edges, fold cuff in half. Matching raw edges and seams, pin cuff to hat; sew in place. Turn hat right-side out. Fold bottom of hat up to form a cuff; randomly sew buttons on cuff. Place hat on snowman.

**Fig. 1**

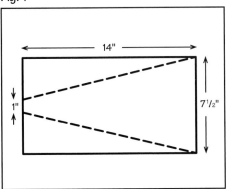

**7.** Slightly fringe the ends of the scarf; tie scarf around snowman's neck.

## PAINTED PLATE

(shown on page 32)

Transform a clear glass plate into a piece of folk-art to match your **Felt Ornaments** and **Garland**.

Trace the heart patterns on page 140 onto a piece of stencil plastic 1" larger all around than each pattern…cut out the hearts along the lines, keeping the outer plastic intact, as this will be your stencil pattern. Marking on the front of the plate, use a marker to divide the plate into quarters. Wipe the back of the plate with alcohol and allow to dry.

Working on the back of the plate, using permanent enamel paint for glass and following the manufacturer's instructions for application and drying time, align the small heart with the marks on the plate; use a 1" diameter spouncer to paint the heart red. Center the larger heart pattern over the red heart and paint purple…don't worry about getting purple on the red because overlapped paint won't show from the front! Use a new pencil eraser to paint green dots along the edges of the purple heart. Repeat to paint hearts at each mark on the plate.

Use the spouncer to paint 1" diameter red circles, evenly spaced between the hearts, around the plate. Paint the back of the plate yellow. Wipe the marks off the front of the plate.

## ETCHED PLATE & GLASS

(shown on page 37)

And you thought you had to be a professional to etch glass!

Apply clear self-adhesive paper to the bottom of a clear glass dinner plate or around a clear glass tumbler…you may need to cut several smaller pieces to apply along the rounded areas so the paper will adhere smoothly. Trace the tree and star patterns from page 140 onto tracing paper, then cut out. Draw around the patterns on the paper adhered to the plate or glass. Leaving the area around the shapes uncut and in place, use a craft knife to cut out the shapes along the drawn lines; remove the shapes.

Following manufacturer's instructions, apply glass-etching cream to the cut-out areas. Remove the paper after the designs are dry.

## STITCHED SANTA AND TEDDY

(shown on page 40)

Refer to *Cross Stitch*, page 131, before beginning project. Use the color key on page 140 for embroidery floss colors.

Using 2 strands of embroidery floss for the *Cross Stitches* and *French Knots* and one strand of floss for the *Backstitches* and *Quarter Stitches*, work the design on page 141 at the center of a 13"x15" piece of 14-count white Aida. When your piece is stitched, frame it as desired.

## PENNY RUG TREE
### Ornaments

(continued from page 43)

For each ornament background, follow manufacturer's instructions to adhere paper-backed fusible web to the wrong side of 2 fabric scraps; trim the scraps to 4 1/2" squares. Leaving the paper backing on the bottom square, layer, then fuse the 2 squares together. Remove the backing from the bottom square.

Trace the desired patterns from pages 146 and 147 onto tracing paper. Using the patterns, cut shapes from felt scraps, then pin them to the background. Referring to the Stitching Key on page 146 and the Stitch Diagrams on the patterns, use 3 strands of coordinating embroidery floss to work the indicated *Embroidery Stitches*, page 132, on the shapes to attach them to the background. Sew on buttons as indicated on the patterns.

Fuse the background to a piece of felt; use pinking shears to trim the felt 1/4" larger on all sides than the background. Use 6 strands of floss to work *Blanket Stitches* along the edges of the background.

For a hanger, sew buttons to the ends of a length of ribbon at the top corners of the ornament.

(continued on page 122)

## Tree Skirt

**1.** For the skirt liner, match right sides and fold a 40" square of checked fabric in half from top to bottom and again from left to right.

**2.** Tie one end of a length of string to a fabric marking pen or pencil. Insert thumbtack through string 19½" inches from the pencil. Insert thumbtack through the fabric as shown in **Fig. 1**; mark the outside cutting line.

**Fig. 1**

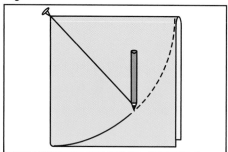

**3.** Repeat Step 2, inserting thumbtack 1" from the pencil; mark the inner cutting line (where the tree trunk goes). Cut through all layers of fabric along the drawn lines.

**4.** Press the outer edge of the liner ¼" to the wrong side; press ¼" to the wrong side again and topstitch in place. Set liner aside for now.

**5.** For the skirt, fold a 37" square of cream-colored felt in half from top to bottom and again from left to right. Using an 18" outer cutting line, follow Step 2 to mark, then cut the skirt. Follow Step 3 to mark and cut the inner cutting line.

**6.** Trace the scallop pattern from page 145 onto tracing paper and cut out. Moving the pattern as necessary, draw scallops along the skirt edges. Cut out the scallops.

**7.** Trace all but the background patterns from page 144 onto tracing paper. Using the patterns, cut one extra-large (use decorative-edge craft scissors to cut it out), one large, 6 medium and 8 small circles from assorted colors of felt; cut 2 large leaves and 8 medium leaves from dark green felt and 34 small leaves from a lighter green felt.

**8.** Referring to the photograph on page 43, the Stitching Key on page 146 and the Stitch Diagrams on the patterns for the Embroidery Stitches, page 132. Pin the felt shapes to the skirt, then use 3 strands of coordinating embroidery floss to work the indicated stitches on each shape and to sew the buttons in place. Use 2 colors of floss, 3 strands each, to work Couch Stitches to connect the flowers and leaves together.

**9.** Matching the inner edges, pin the skirt on the liner. Cut a straight-line opening through liner and skirt from inner circle to outer edges between 2 scallops. Using 6 strands of floss, work Blanket Stitches along the edges of the skirt; working through the skirt and liner, work Blanket Stitches around the inner circle and the skirt opening.

## MANTEL SCARF
(shown on pages 44 and 45)

**1.** For the liner, measure the depth of the mantel, including the thickness and desired drop length, then the width of the mantel. Add 1" to each measurement; cut a piece of fabric the determined measurements. Press all sides of the liner ¼" to the wrong side, then press ¼" to the wrong side again; topstitch in place. Set aside for now.

**2.** For the scalloped topper, subtract 1" from the determined mantel width measurement and 2" from the depth measurement; cut a piece of felt the determined measurements.

**3.** Size the scallop pattern from page 145 on a photocopier as necessary for an even number of scallops to fit across the topper; use the pattern to cut scallops along the front edge of the topper. Using 6 strands of embroidery floss, work Blanket Stitches, page 132, along the scalloped edge.

**4.** Trace all but the background patterns from page 144 onto tracing paper. Using the patterns, cut one extra-large (use decorative-edge craft scissors to cut it out), one large, 6 medium and 8 small circles from assorted colors of felt; cut 2 large leaves and 8 medium leaves from dark green felt and 34 small leaves from a lighter green felt.

**5.** Referring to the photograph on pages 44 and 45 for placement, the Stitching Key on page 146 and the Stitch Diagram on the patterns for the Embroidery Stitches, page 132, pin the felt shapes to the topper, then use 3 strands of coordinating embroidery floss to work the indicated stitches on each shape and to sew the buttons in place. Use 3 strands each of 2 colors of floss to work Couch Stitches to connect the flowers and leaves together.

**6.** Matching back and side edges of the liner and topper, working through liner and topper and using 6 strands of embroidery floss, work Blanket Stitches along the back and sides of the scarf.

## FRAMED HANDPRINT
(shown on page 51)

You can't keep those tiny hands small forever, but you can remember how precious they were when you capture an impression of them in this shadowbox, complete with photograph and nameplate.

Allow glue, primer and paint to dry after each application.

Select fabric and acrylic paint to coordinate with the photograph to be displayed in a wooden shadowbox. Glue the fabric to the back of the box. Apply primer, then the selected paint to the frame.

Mix one part water with one part white acrylic paint; apply a light coat of the mixture to the frame...additional coats may be necessary for the desired coverage.

Following manufacturer's instructions to knead and dry, work white modeling compound into a ¾" thick oval shape large enough to accommodate the child's hand. Make the hand impression and allow to dry.

Draw around the photograph on decorative paper or card stock; cut out ¼" inside the drawn line, then use decorative-edge craft scissors to cut out ½" outside the drawn line to make a frame.

Arrange, then glue the impression and photograph to the back of the box; glue the frame to the photograph.

Use a fine-point marker to write the name and date on a metal-trimmed inventory tag; glue the tag in place.

## GIFT WRAP IDEAS

(shown on pages 54 and 55)

Festive wraps and handmade tags add your personal touch to the holidays. You can refer to *Making a Tag or Label*, page 132, for some tag tips from your Country Friends®.

Wrap boxes in handmade paper and tie closed with raffia for a simple gift wrap…be sure to add a sticker-lettered nametag to show who it belongs to. If the paper is kind of plain, liven it up by stamping a simple holly design on it…glue on buttons for the berries and add wire-edged net ribbon.

Or, for originality, weave strips of sheer ribbon over the top of the package (glue the ends to the bottom to secure)…add a 2-layer heart-shaped tag outlined with miniature holly.

This little reindeer bag is easy to make and fun to give. Place your gift in the bag, then fold the top of the bag into a pointed flap (this is the head). Glue a big brown shank button to the end point of the flap for a nose…glue it at the very tip so the glue will adhere the head to the bag and the nose will cover the glue. Glue 2 black buttons for eyes (paint a white highlight on each eye) above the nose. Cut out 2 ear shapes from plush felt and glue one end of each ear to the back corners of the head; glue 2 twig antlers to the back of the head. For a collar, glue the ends of a piece of ribbon to the sides of the bag, then sew a jingle bell to the center of the ribbon. Hang a tag from the antlers.

For the stocking decoration, trace the patterns from page 148 onto tracing paper and cut out. Using the patterns, cut a small stocking from felt and a cuff from plush felt…use decorative-edge craft scissors to cut a large stocking and 2 squares from handmade paper. Arrange and glue the cut-outs together, sew a jingle bell to the toe of the stocking, then use stickers to spell out the name on the cuff.

## SANTA MEMORY ALBUM

(shown on page 59)

- 3-ring photo album
- wallpaper
- spray adhesive
- hot glue gun
- white card stock
- clear plastic
- paper maché frame to fit front of album (with stand removed)
- Santa rubber stamp
- color pencils
- handmade paper
- decorative vellum

*Use hot glue for all gluing unless otherwise indicated.*

**1.** To cover album, draw around open album on wrong side of wallpaper; cut out wallpaper 2" outside drawn lines. Apply spray adhesive to wrong side of wallpaper piece; center open album on wallpaper piece. Close album; smooth wallpaper piece on front and back of album. Reopen album…fold corners of wallpaper diagonally over corners of album. Trimming and clipping wallpaper to fit under binding hardware, fold edges of wallpaper over edges of album and glue in place.

**2.** To cover insides of album, measure inside height of album; subtract $1/2$". Measure front inside width from edge of album to edge of binding hardware, then subtract $1/2$"; cut a piece of wallpaper the determined measurements. Apply spray adhesive to wrong side of wallpaper piece; center and smooth over inside front of album. Repeat to cover inside back of album.

**3.** Cut a piece of card stock and clear plastic to fit in frame. Place the card stock in the frame; stamp a Santa on the card stock. Use colored pencils to color the Santa. Place plastic in the frame over the card stock.

**4.** Tear a piece of handmade paper $1/2$" larger on all sides than the frame; center and glue to front of album. Cut a piece of vellum 2" larger on all sides than the frame. Center vellum piece, right-side up, on frame; use a pencil to draw around opening in frame, then cut out opening. Apply spray adhesive to wrong side of vellum piece. Aligning openings, smooth vellum onto frame, then edges to back of frame. Center and glue frame on handmade paper on front of album.

## VINTAGE PILLOWS

(shown on pages 60 and 61)

Lavishly embellish throw pillows with bits & pieces of this & that you've crocheted, sewn, embroidered or collected through the years…pot holders, tatted trim, hankies, doilies. If you don't have those things to decorate with, just cut and hem strips and bands from dish towels…tack them around pillows, then adorn with coordinating buttons!

Or, if you don't have lots of pillows to decorate, that's no problem…they're really quick & easy to make. Just cut 2 pieces of fabric the same size, match the right sides and edges, then sew the pieces together…leave a small opening for turning and stuffing with fiberfill, or a larger opening to accommodate a pillow form. Turn right-side out, fill with fiberfill or a pillow form, then sew the opening closed.

You can also create a pillow from a pretty pillowcase. Add a ruffle or 2 to the open end of the pillowcase; remove the wire from one edge of a length of wired ribbon ($2^1/2$ times the width of the pillowcase), gather the other edge to fit around the opening, then sew in place. Or, cut a 9" wide strip of fabric ($2^1/2$ times the width of the pillowcase), hem the short edges, then fold the strip in half lengthwise, matching long edges and wrong sides. Baste along the raw edges, pull the threads to gather ruffle to fit around pillowcase opening and sew in place. Sew trim over the stitching line made from sewing on the ruffle, then sew braid or cord along the edge of the trim. Insert a pillow form in the case, then fold the top of the case over for a flap…spot tack if desired.

# BOY'S HAT AND SCARF

(shown on page 62)

*Refer to Crochet, page 130, before beginning project.*

**See How to Measure Child's Head, page 130.**

| SIZES | MEASUREMENTS | |
|---|---|---|
| | Head | Hat |
| Small | 16" (40.5 cm) | 15" (38 cm) |
| Medium | 17" (43 cm) | 16" (40.5 cm) |
| Large | 18" (47.5 cm) | 17" (43 cm) |

| SIZES (without fringe) | MEASUREMENTS Scarf (wide x length) |
|---|---|
| Small | 5¹/₂" x 38" (14 cm x 96.5 cm) |
| Medium | 6¹/₄ x 43" (16 cm x 109 cm) |
| Large | 7" x 48" (18 cm x 122 cm) |

**Size Note:** *Instructions are written for size Small, with sizes Medium and Large in braces { }. Instructions will be easier to read if you circle all the numbers that pertain to your size. If only one number is given, it applies to all sizes.*

## MATERIALS
### Hat & Scarf Set Total
Worsted Weight Yarn:
MC (Grey)
Ounces    4¹/₂{5³/₄-7¹/₄}
Yards    295{350-435}
Grams    130{165-205}
Meters    269.5{320-398}
CC (Scraps) **total**
Ounces    4¹/₂{5³/₄-7¹/₄}
Yards    295{350-435}
Grams    130{165-205}
Meters    269.5{320-398}

### Hat
Worsted Weight Yarn:
MC (Grey)
Ounces    2{2¹/₄-2¹/₂}
Yards    130{150-165}
Grams    60{65-70}
Meters    119{137-151}
CC (Scraps) **total**
Ounces    2{2¹/₄-2¹/₂}
Yards    130{150-165}
Grams    60{65-70}
Meters    119{137-151}

## Scarf
Worsted Weight Yarn:
MC (Grey)
Ounces    2¹/₂{3¹/₂-4³/₄}
Yards    165{200-270}
Grams    70{100-135}
Meters    151{183-247}
CC (Scraps) **total**
Ounces    2¹/₂{3¹/₂-4³/₄}
Yards    165{200-270}
Grams    70{100-135}
Meters    151{183-247}
Crochet hook, size I (5.5 mm) **or** size needed for gauge
Yarn needle

**Note about fringe:** *Each row is worked across length of Hat **and** Scarf. When joining yarn **and** finishing off, leave a 6" (15 cm) length to be worked in with pom-pom on Hat **and** fringe on Scarf.*

**GAUGE:** 11 sc and 13 rows of ribbing = 3" (7.5 cm)

**Gauge Swatch:** 3" (7.5 cm) square

## Hat & Scarf
Ch 12 **loosely.**

**Row 1** (Right side): Sc in second ch from hook and in each ch across: 11 sc.

**Rows 2-13:** Ch 1, turn; sc in Back Loop Only of first sc and each sc across **(Fig. 2, page 130).**

Finish off.

## HAT
With MC, ch 40{46-50}.

**Row 1** (Wrong side): Sc in second ch from hook and in next 4{6-8} chs, ★ ch 1, skip next ch, sc in next ch; repeat from ★ across; finish off: 22{26-29} sc.

**Note #1:** *Loop a short piece of yarn around **back** of any stitch to mark **right** side.*

**Note #2:** *Work in Back Loops Only throughout **(Fig. 2, page 130).***

**Row 2:** With **right** side facing, join CC with sc in first sc **(see Joining With Sc, page 130);** ch 1, (sc in next sc, ch 1) across to last 5{7-9} sc, sc in last 5{7-9} sc.

**Row 3:** Ch 1, turn; sc in first 5{7-9} sc, (ch 1, sc in next sc) across; finish off.

**Row 4:** With **right** side facing, join MC with sc in first sc; ch 1, (sc in next sc, ch 1) across to last 5{7-9} sc, sc in last 5{7-9} sc.

**Row 5:** Ch 1, turn; sc in first 5{7-9} sc, (ch 1, sc in next sc) across; finish off.

**Row 6:** With **right** side facing, join CC with sc in first sc; ch 1, (sc in next sc, ch 1) across to last 5{7-9} sc, sc in last 5{7-9} sc.

**Row 7:** Ch 1, turn; sc in first 5{7-9} sc, (ch 1, sc in next sc) across; finish off.

Repeat Rows 4-7 until ribbing measures 15{16-17}"/38{40.5-43} cm, ending by working Row 6.

Finish off, leaving a long end for sewing.

### FINISHING
Thread yarn needle with long end. Fold Hat with **right** side together, matching sts and working in *Free Loops* of beginning ch **(Fig. 4, page 130)** and inside loops of sts on last row, insert the needle from back to front through first stitch and pull yarn through. ★ insert the needle from back to front through next stitch and pull yarn through; repeat from ★ across. With **right** side facing and keeping yarn ends to **right** side of Hat, weave yarn end through one loop at the end of every other row at top of Hat; gather **tightly** and secure end.

### POM-POM
Cut a piece of cardboard 3" (7.5 cm) wide and as long as you want the diameter of your finished pom-pom to be.

Holding one strand of **each** color together, make pom-pom. Wind the yarn lengthwise around the cardboard until it is about one inch thick in the middle **(Fig. 1).**

Carefully slip the yarn off the cardboard and firmly tie an 18" (45.5 cm) length of yarn around the middle **(Fig. 2).** Leave yarn ends long enough to attach the pom-pom. Cut the loops on both ends and trim the pom-pom into a smooth ball.

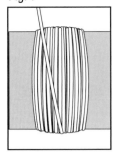

Fig. 1

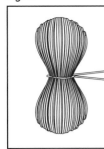

Fig. 2

Sew pom-pom in center of yarn ends and secure. Gather yarn ends at base of pom-pom and secure **tightly** with a 6" (15.25 cm) piece of yarn. Trim yarn ends to blend in with pom-pom.

Turn ribbing up.

## SCARF

With MC, ch 160{184-200}.

**Row 1** (Right side): Working in *Back Ridge* of beginning ch (**Fig. 3, page 130**), sc in second ch from hook, ★ ch 1, skip next ch, sc in next ch; repeat from ★ across; finish off: 80{92-100} sc.

**Note #1:** Loop a short piece of yarn around any stitch to mark Row 1 as **right** side.

**Note #2:** Work in Back Loops Only throughout (**Fig. 2, page 130**).

**Row 2:** Ch 1, turn; sc in first sc, (ch 1, sc in next sc) across; finish off.

**Row 3:** With **right** side facing, join CC with sc in first sc (**see Joining With Sc, page 130**); (ch 1, sc in next sc) across.

**Row 4:** Ch 1, turn; sc in first sc, (ch 1, sc in next sc) across; finish off.

**Row 5:** With **right** side facing, join MC with sc in first sc; (ch 1, sc in next sc) across.

**Row 6:** Ch 1, turn; sc in first sc, (ch 1, sc in next sc) across; finish off.

**Row 7:** With **right** side facing, join CC with sc in first sc; (ch 1, sc in next sc) across.

**Row 8:** Ch 1, turn; sc in first sc, (ch 1, sc in next sc) across; finish off.

Repeat Rows 5-8 until scarf measures 5½{6¼-7}"/14{16-17.75} cm, ending by working Row 8.

For Scarf end **with** yarn ends, holding together 5{6-7} 12" strands of MC **and** one strand of corresponding color, add Fringe evenly spaced across short edges of Scarf in end of rows (**Figs. 5c & 5d, page 130**).

For Scarf end **without** yarn ends, holding together 4{5-6} 12" strands of MC **and** two strands of corresponding color, add fringe evenly spaced across short edges of Scarf in end of rows (**Figs. 5c & 5d, page 130**).

## GIRL'S HAT AND SCARF

(shown on page 63)
**See How to Measure Child's Head, page 130.**

| SIZES | MEASUREMENTS | |
|---|---|---|
| | Head | Hat |
| Small | 16" (40.5 cm) | 14¾" (37.5 cm) |
| Medium | 17" (43 cm) | 16" (40.5 cm) |
| Large | 18" (45.5 cm) | 17½" (44.5 cm) |

| SIZES (without fringe) | MEASUREMENTS Scarf (wide x length) |
|---|---|
| Small | 5½" x 40" (14 cm x 101.5 cm) |
| Medium | 6" x 44" (15 cm x 112 cm) |
| Large | 6½" x 48"(16.5 cm x 122 cm) |

**Size Note:** Instructions are written for size Small, with sizes Medium and Large in braces { }. Instructions will be easier to read if you circle all the numbers that pertain to your child's size. If only one number is given, it applies to all sizes.

## MATERIALS
### Hat & Scarf Set Total
Baby Fingering Weight Yarn:
Blue

| | |
|---|---|
| Ounces | 3½{4-4½} |
| Yards | 190{210-235} |
| Grams | 100{110-130} |
| Meters | 173.5{192-215} |

White

| | |
|---|---|
| Ounces | 2{2½-3} |
| Yards | 110{135-195} |
| Grams | 55{70-90} |
| Meters | 100.5{123.5-178.5} |

### Hat
Baby Fingering Weight Yarn:
Blue

| | |
|---|---|
| Ounces | 1{1¼-1½} |
| Yards | 30{35-45} |
| Grams | 30{35-40} |
| Meters | 27.5{32-41} |

White

| | |
|---|---|
| Ounces | ½{¾-1} |
| Yards | 15{25-65} |
| Grams | 15{20-30} |
| Meters | 13.5{23-59.5} |

### Scarf
Baby Fingering Weight Yarn:
Blue

| | |
|---|---|
| Ounces | 2½{2¾-3} |
| Yards | 160{175-190} |
| Grams | 70{80-90} |
| Meters | 146.5{160-173.5} |

White

| | |
|---|---|
| Ounces | 1½{1¾-2} |
| Yards | 95{110-130} |
| Grams | 40{50-60} |
| Meters | 87{100.5-119} |

Crochet hook, size indicated **or** size needed for gauge

| | |
|---|---|
| Small | B (3 mm) |
| Medium | D (3.25 mm) |
| Large | F (3.75 mm) |

Tapestry needle
**GAUGE:** Square A (Rnds 1-4) = 2½{2¾-3}"
6.25{7-7.5}cm
**Gauge Swatch:** Work same as Rnds 1-4 on Square A.

## STITCH GUIDE
Treble Crochet (abbreviated **tr**)
YO twice, insert hook in sp indicated, YO and pull up a loop (4 loops on hook), (YO and draw through 2 loops on hook) 3 times.

Picot
Ch 3, slip st in third ch from hook.

Cluster
★ YO, insert hook in st indicated, YO and pull up a loop, YO and draw through 2 loops on hook; repeat from ★ once **more**, YO and draw through all 3 loops on hook.

Puff St
★ YO, insert hook in st or sp indicated, YO and pull up a loop even with loop on hook; repeat from ★ 3 times **more** (9 loops on hook), YO and draw through first 8 loops on hook, YO and draw through remaining 2 loops on hook.

*(continued on page 126)*

**Decrease** (uses next 3 dc)

YO, † insert hook in next dc, YO and pull up a loop, YO and draw through 2 loops on hook †, YO, skip next dc, repeat from † to † once, YO and draw through all 3 loops on hook (**counts as one dc**).

**Front Post Double Crochet** (abbreviated **FPdc**)

YO, insert hook from **front** to **back** around post of st indicated (**Fig. 3**), YO and pull up a loop, (YO and draw through 2 loops on hook) twice. Skip st **behind** FPdc.

**Fig. 3**

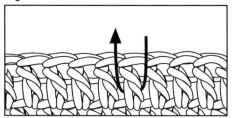

## HAT BODY
### SQUARE A (Make 3)

With White, ch 4; join with slip st to form a ring.

**Rnd 1** (Right side): Ch 2, 16 hdc in ring; skip beginning ch-2; join with slip st to next hdc: 16 hdc.

*Note: Loop a short piece of yarn around any stitch to mark Rnd 1 as **right** side.*

**Rnd 2:** Ch 2, work (dc, Picot, Cluster) in same st (**ch-2 and first dc count as Beginning Cluster, now and throughout**), ch 3, skip next hdc, ★ work (Cluster, Picot, Cluster) in next hdc, ch 3, skip next hdc; repeat from ★ around; join with slip st to Beginning Cluster, finish off: 8 ch-3 sps.

**Rnd 3:** With **right** side facing, join Blue with dc in any ch-3 sp (**see Joining With Dc, page 130**); (tr, ch 2, tr, dc) in same sp, ch 2, (hdc, sc, hdc) in next ch-3 sp, ch 2, ★ (dc, tr, ch 2, tr, dc) in next ch-3 sp, ch 2, (hdc, sc, hdc) in next ch-3 sp, ch 2; repeat from ★ 2 times **more**; join with slip st to first dc: 28 sts and 12 ch-2 sps.

**Rnd 4:** Ch 1, sc in same st and in next tr, ★ † (sc, hdc, sc) in corner ch-2 sp, sc in next 2 sts, 2 sc in next ch-2 sp, sc in next 3 sts, 2 sc in next ch-2 sp †, sc in next 2 sts; repeat from ★ 2 times **more**, then repeat from † to † once; join with slip st to first sc, finish off: 56 sts.

**Trim:** With **right** side facing, join Blue with hdc in any corner hdc (**see Joining With Hdc, page 130**); hdc in next sc and in each st across working last hdc in next corner hdc; finish off: 15 hdc.

Work Trim in same manner on opposite side of Square, finish off leaving a long end for sewing.

### SQUARE B (Make 2)

With White, ch 4; join with slip st to form a ring.

**Rnd 1** (Right side): Ch 2, (work Puff St in ring, ch 2) 8 times; skip beginning ch-2 and join with slip st to first Puff St: 8 Puff Sts.

*Note: Mark Rnd 1 as **right** side.*

**Rnd 2:** Ch 2, (work Puff St in same st, ch 2) twice, work Puff St in next Puff St, ch 2, ★ (work Puff St, ch 2) twice in next Puff St, work Puff St in next Puff St, ch 2; repeat from ★ 2 times **more**; skip beginning ch-2 and join with slip st to first Puff St, finish off: 12 Puff Sts.

**Rnd 3:** With **right** side facing, join Blue with sc in same st as joining (**see Joining With Sc, page 130**); ch 2, sc in next Puff St, ch 3, (dc, ch 3) twice in next Puff St, ★ sc in next Puff St, ch 2, sc in next Puff St, ch 3, (dc, ch 3) twice in next Puff St; repeat from ★ 2 times **more**; join with slip st to first sc: 16 sts and 16 sps.

**Rnd 4:** Ch 1, sc in same st, ★ † working **around** next ch-2 sp, dc in ch-2 sp one rnd **below**, sc in next sc, working **around** next ch-3 sp, 2 dc in ch-2 sp one rnd **below**, sc in next dc, (2 sc, hdc, 2 sc) in corner ch-3 sp, sc in next dc, working **around** next ch-3 sp, 2 dc in ch-2 sp one rnd **below** †, sc in next sc; repeat from ★ 2 times **more**, then repeat from † to † once; join with slip st to first sc, finish off: 56 sts.

Work Trim in same manner as Square A.

## ASSEMBLY

Join Squares in the following order: A, B, A, B, and A.

Using Blue and working through **both** loops, sew Squares together along Trims to form a strip, beginning in first hdc and ending in last hdc; then sew ends of strip together in same manner to form a ring.

*Note: Mark joining between adjacent Square A pieces as center back of Cap.*

## EDGING

With **right** side facing and working across one long edge of Hat Body, join Blue with sc in center back joining; sc in end of next Trim, ★ † working across next Square, sc in first corner hdc and in each st across to next corner hdc on same Square, sc in corner hdc and in end of next Trim †, sc in joining and in end of next Trim; repeat from ★ 3 times **more**, then repeat from † to †; join with slip st to first sc, finish off: 90 sc.

## CROWN

With Blue, ch 3; join with slip st to form a ring.

**Rnd 1:** Ch 3 (**counts as first dc, now and throughout**), 14 dc in ring; join with slip st to first dc: 15 dc.

*Note: Mark Rnd 1 as **right** side.*

**Rnd 2:** Ch 3, (2 dc in next dc, dc in next dc) around; join with slip st to first dc, finish off: 22 dc.

**Rnd 3:** With **right** side facing, join White with slip st in same st as joining; ch 2, work (dc, Picot, Cluster) in same st, ch 2, skip next dc, ★ work (Cluster, Picot, Cluster) in next dc, ch 2, skip next dc; repeat from ★ around; join with slip st to Beginning Cluster, finish off: 11 ch-2 sps.

**Rnd 4:** With **right** side facing, join Blue with dc in last ch-2 sp **before** joining; 2 dc in same sp, ch 1, (3 dc in next ch-2 sp, ch 1) around; join with slip st to first dc: 33 dc and 11 ch-1 sps.

**Rnd 5:** Ch 3, 2 dc in next dc, dc in next dc, 2 dc in next ch-1 sp, (dc in next 3 dc, 2 dc in next ch-1 sp) around; join with slip st to first dc, finish off: 56 dc.

**Rnd 6:** With **right** side facing, join White with slip st in same st as joining; ch 4 (**counts as first dc plus ch 1**), dc in same st, ★ † skip next dc, work Puff St in next dc, ch 1, decrease, ch 1, work Puff St in next dc, skip next dc †, (dc, ch 1, dc) in next dc; repeat from ★ 5 times **more**, then repeat from † to † once; join with slip st to first dc, finish off: 14 Puff Sts, 21 dc and 21 ch-1 sps.

**Rnd 7:** With **right** side facing, join Blue with dc in first ch-1 sp **after** joining; ★ † skip next dc, dc in sp **before** next Puff St, work FPdc around top of next Puff St, dc in sp **before** next dc, dc in next dc and in sp **before** next Puff St, work FPdc around top of next Puff St, dc in sp **before** next dc †, dc in next ch-1 sp; repeat from ★ 5 times **more**, then repeat from † to † once; join with slip st to first dc: 56 sts.

**Rnd 8:** Ch 3, dc in same st and in next 3 sts, (2 dc in next dc, dc in next 3 sts) around; join with slip st to first dc: 70 dc.

**Rnd 9:** Ch 3, dc in next 2 dc, 2 dc in next dc, (dc in next 4 dc, 2 dc in next dc) around to last dc, dc in last dc; join with slip st to first dc, finish off: 84 dc.

**Rnd 10:** With **right** side facing, join White with sc in same st as joining; sc in next 12 dc, 2 sc in next dc, (sc in next 13 dc, 2 sc in next dc) around; join with slip st to first sc, finish off leaving a long end for sewing: 90 sc.

Thread tapestry needle with long end. Working through **both** loops and matching Crown joining to center back joining, whipstitch Crown to Body Edging.

### BRIM

**Rnd 1:** With **right** side facing and working along bottom edge of Body, join Blue with sc in first corner hdc on Square **after** center back joining; sc in each st across to next corner hdc on same Square, sc in corner hdc, 2 sc in end of each of next 2 Trims, ★ working across next Square, sc in first corner hdc and in each st across to next corner hdc on same Square, sc in corner hdc, 2 sc in end of each of next 2 Trims; repeat from ★ around; join with slip st to first sc, finish off: 95 sc.

**Rnd 2:** With **right** side facing, join White with sc in same st as joining; sc in next 15 sc, 2 sc in next sc, (sc in next 18 sc, 2 sc in next sc) around to last 2 sc, sc in last 2 sc; join with slip st to first sc: 100 sc.

**Rnd 3:** Ch 1, 2 sc in same st, sc in next 9 sc, (2 sc in next sc, sc in next 9 sc) around; join with slip st to first sc, finish off: 110 sc.

**Rnd 4:** With **right** side facing, join Blue with dc in same st as joining; dc in next sc and in each sc around; join with slip st to first dc.

**Rnds 5-7:** Ch 3, dc in next dc and in each dc around; join with slip st to first dc. Finish off.

**Rnd 8:** With **right** side facing, join White with slip st in same st as joining; ch 1, (slip st in next dc, ch 1) around; join with slip st to first slip st, finish off.

## SCARF

### CENTER

### SQUARE A (Make 6)

Work same as Hat Body Square A.

### SQUARE B (Make 7)

Work same as Hat Body Square B.

### ASSEMBLY

Join Squares in the following order: A, (B, A) 6 times.

Using Blue and working through **both** loops, whipstitch Squares together along Trims to form a strip, beginning in first hdc and ending in last hdc.

### BORDER

**Row 1:** With **right** side facing and working across one long edge of Scarf, join Blue with sc in end of first Trim; sc in same Trim, working across next Square, sc in first corner hdc and in each st across to next corner hdc on same Square, ★ sc in corner hdc and in end of next Trim, sc in joining and in end of next Trim, working across next Square, sc in first corner hdc and in each st across to next corner hdc on same Square; repeat from ★ once **more**, sc in corner hdc, † 2 sc in end of each of next 2 Trims, working across next Square, sc in first corner hdc and in each st across to next corner hdc on same Square, sc in corner hdc †; repeat from † to † across to last Trim, 2 sc in end of last Trim; finish off: 245 sc.

**Row 2:** With **right** side facing, join White with sc in first sc; sc in next sc and in each sc across.

**Row 3:** Ch 1, turn; sc in each sc across; finish off.

**Row 4:** With **right** side facing, join Blue with dc in first sc; dc in next sc and in each sc across.

**Row 5:** Ch 3, turn; dc in next dc and in each dc across; finish off.

**Row 6:** With **right** side facing, join White with dc in first dc; ch 1, decrease, ch 1, ★ work Puff St in next dc, skip next dc, (dc, ch 1, dc) in next dc, skip next dc, work Puff St in next dc, ch 1, decrease, ch 1; repeat from ★ across to last dc, dc in last dc; finish off: 60 Puff Sts, 93 dc and 92 ch-1 sps.

Work Border in same manner on opposite long edge of Scarf.

### EDGING

***Note:*** *To change colors, work sc indicated to within one step of completion, hook new yarn and draw through both loops on hook* **(Fig. 4)**. *Use a separate small ball of yarn at each short edge of Scarf and cut yarn when instructed. When working over unused color, hold yarn with normal tension and keep it to* **wrong** *side of work.*

**Fig. 4**

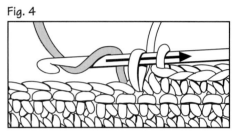

**Rnd 1:** With **right** side facing, join Blue with sc in first dc on one long edge; sc in same st and in next ch-1 sp, † sc in next dc and in next ch-1 sp, ★ sc in next Puff St and in sp **before** next dc, sc in next ch-1 sp, skip next dc, sc in sp before next Puff St, sc in next Puff St and in next ch-1 sp, sc in next dc and in next ch-1 sp; repeat from ★ across to last dc, 2 sc in last dc changing to White in last sc made, sc in same st; working in end of rows, 2 sc in same row changing to Blue in last sc made, 2 sc in each of next 2 rows changing to White in last sc made, sc in next 2 rows changing to Blue in last sc made, sc in next row, working across Trim, sc in same hdc as sc at end of Row 1 on Border, sc in each hdc across, sc in same hdc as sc at end of Row 1 on opposite Border, working in end of rows, sc in next row changing to White, sc in next 2 rows changing to Blue in last sc made, 2 sc in each of next 2 rows changing to White in last sc made, 2 sc in last row †; working across long edge, sc in first dc changing to Blue, cut White, 2 sc in same st, sc in next ch-1 sp, repeat from † to † once, sc in same st as first sc changing to Blue, cut White; join with slip st to first sc.

*(continued on page 128)*

**Rnd 2:** Ch 1, 2 sc in same st, † sc in next sc and in each sc across to center sc of next corner 3-sc group, 2 sc in center sc, ch 1, skip next sc, ★ sc in next sc, ch 1, skip next sc; repeat from ★ across to center sc of next corner 3-sc group †, 2 sc in center sc, repeat from † to † once; join with slip st to first sc, finish off.

**Trim:** With **right** side facing and working across one long edge of Scarf, join White with slip st in first sc of first corner 2-sc group; (ch 1, slip st in next sc) across working last slip st in second sc of next corner 2-sc group; finish off.

Work Trim in same manner on opposite long edge of Scarf.

Holding 4 strands of corresponding color together, each 12" long, add Fringe in each ch-1 sp across short edges of Scarf **(Figs. 5a & 5b, page 130)**.

## LUGGAGE TAGS
(shown on page 67)

These tags are fun to make...and they'll help your favorite guy keep up with his belongings!.

Cut a tag from plain or decorative card stock. Either stamp or use stickers to spell out the name and address on the tag. Select stickers or scrapbook embellishments to set the mood for the tag, then glue them in place on the tag. Use fine-point paint pens to add any handlettered or drawn details to the tag.

Cover the front and back of the tag with self-adhesive laminating sheets (there are several textures to choose from), then trim it 1/4" larger on all sides than the tag.

Punch a hole in the tag and use small cord to attach it to the item it needs to identify.

## "SEASON'S GREETINGS" WALL HANGING
(continued from page 68)

**5.** Trace the word patterns, page 151, onto tissue paper. Arrange and pin the paper on the ground snow. Stitching through the paper, work Backstitches along the drawn lines; carefully remove the paper.

**6.** Fold each hanging strip in half and glue the ends together. Spacing evenly, glue the loops to the top back side of the wall hanging. Thread a stick from the yard through the loops. For a hanger, knot the ends of a length of jute around the ends of the stick. Tie and glue a jute bow to each corner square on the wall hanging.

## DECORATED CARDBOARD BAG
(shown on page 74)

Measure around a corrugated cardboard bag with handles, then cut a piece of jumbo rick-rack just longer than the determined measurement. Use embroidery floss to attach E and leaf-shaped beads to the bumps along the bottom edge of the rick-rack. Glue the rick-rack around the bag.

For the nametag ornament, drill a hole through a wooden circle cut-out. Paint the ornament yellow, then green (allow the paint to dry after each applications). Very lightly sand the center and the edges of the circle, then wipe with a tack cloth. Use alphabet stickers to spell out your message, then use a piece of jute to attach it to the handle on the bag.

## SNOWMAN PLATE
(shown on page 75)

This adorable plate is quick & simple to make, but remember to hand wash it so the motifs won't come off.

Sizing to fit the bottom of a clear glass plate, photocopy the snowman from page 154 onto white card stock; trace the hat, brim, ball and scarf patterns onto tracing paper. Cut out the snowman and patterns.

Use the patterns to cut shapes from decorated paper, then glue them to the snowman...center and glue the snowman to a piece of snowflake-motif paper. Centering the snowman, cut out a circle around the snowman to fit the plate bottom; glue to the bottom side of the plate. Cut out a few snowflakes from the paper and glue them to the underside of the rim.

## MITTEN GIFTS
(shown on page 77)

For a 2-gift-in-one idea, tuck a bag of yummy goodies inside cozy warm winter mittens!

If you want to make the "bags" extra special, use yarn to tie on jingle bells, or clear thread to attach miniature doilies with jingle bells centered on them, to the mittens. Weave wire-edged Christmasy ribbon along the fold of the cuff, then tie the ribbon into a bow.

## PAINTED SHAKER BOX
(shown on page 79)

Need a handy container to tote several gifts in at once? Paint a round wooden Shaker box red, then green...allow the paint to dry after each application. Lightly sand some of the green paint away for an aged look. Line the box with natural excelsior and fill with individual bags stuffed with goodies.

## LINED GIFT BASKET
(shown on page 80)

- wicker basket with handle
- homespun for liner, bag and tag
- 3/8" wide grosgrain ribbon
- clear nylon thread
- red 1/2" long wooden beads
- 4 yellow wooden star buttons
- decorative-edge craft scissors
- red and natural card stock
- paper-backed fusible web
- black fine-point permanent marker
- craft glue
- 4 yellow star-shaped stickers
- jute

**1.** Referring to **Fig. 1** and measuring along the outside of the basket, measure length (A) and width (B) of basket; add 3" to each measurement. Cut a piece of homespun the determined measurements.

**Fig. 1**

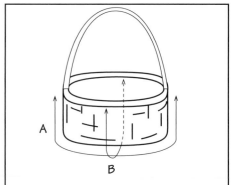

**2.** Matching short edges, fold fabric piece in half and crease fold; unfold fabric and place wrong-side up on a flat surface. To notch liner for handle, place the center of the basket handle along crease in fabric; beginning at edge of fabric, mark a 3" long dotted fold line on fabric along each side of the handle. Remove basket. Starting from edge of fabric, draw along crease 2¹/₂"; connect the end of the drawn line to the ends of the 3" lines, forming a Y (**Fig. 2**). Cut along drawn lines, fold each flap to the wrong side along dotted fold line and sew in place. Repeat for opposite side of crease.

**Fig. 2**

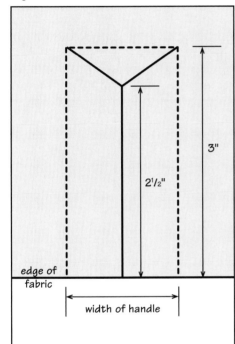

**3.** For a casing, fold remaining raw edges ¹/₂" to the wrong side and sew in place. Tuck ¹/₂" of each length of ribbon into each casing opening and sew to secure. Use nylon thread to sew beads along the hem and to sew one star to each side of the basket below the handle. Place the liner in the basket, overlapping 3" to the outside. Tie the ribbon lengths on each side of the basket into a bow.

**4.** Glue a length of ribbon along the center of the handle. Thread the star buttons onto a length of nylon thread, then thread several red beads onto each side of the stars; tie the ends of the thread around the handle.

**5.** For the bag, cut an 8"x22" piece of homespun. Fold short edges ³/₄" to the wrong side twice, then sew in place. Matching right sides and short edges, fold homespun in half; sew edges together. Turn bag right-side out.

**6.** For the recipe tag, use craft scissors to cut a 5"x6" background from red card stock. Fuse web to the back of a scrap of homespun left from the liner; trim to 4¹/₂"x5¹/₂", then fuse to the center of the background. Use the marker to write the recipe on page 80 and draw a border onto a 3¹/₂"x4¹/₂" piece of natural card stock; glue to the center of the homespun piece. Adhere one star sticker at each corner of the tag. Punch 2 holes through the top of the tag.

**7.** Fill the bag with scone mix. To attach the tag to the bag, wrap jute around the top of the bag once, then thread one side of the tag and 5 beads onto the jute, thread jute through remaining hole in tag, around bag and into a bow.

## SNOWFLAKE CONTAINER
(shown on page 83)

Photocopy the cooking instructions label from page 155 onto white card stock; cut out just outside of the photocopied lines. Use crayons, markers or colored pencils to color the label, then use clear glue to adhere it to an air-tight, clear acrylic container. Place the gift mix in the container. Gluing ends to secure, wrap satin ribbons around the container, then adhere white snowflake stickers to the ribbon and container.

## KIDS' TAGS
(shown on page 84)

Photocopy the desired tag from page 156 onto card stock. Let the kids use crayons, markers or colored pencils to color the tag, then glue it to a Christmasy colored piece of card stock; use decorative-edge craft scissors to trim the card stock ¹/₄" larger on all sides than the tag, then punch a hole at the top.

Place goodies the kids have made in a cellophane bag and tie it closed with a jumbo pipe cleaner. Slide one of the tags, then a few Christmasy colors of sunburst sequins onto the pipe cleaner...add a tiny red jingle bell to each end of the pipe cleaner, then curl the pipe cleaner as desired.

## STICKERED SOUP MUG
(shown on page 85)

Whether making this oh-so simple mug for themselves or to give as a gift, kids of all ages will be pleased with their own special holiday dish.

To decorate the mug (hand wash it only please!), simply adhere stickers to it as desired...we used stripe, snowball, snowflake and mitten stickers.

For the recipe card, use decorative-edge craft scissors to cut a 3"x4¹/₂" piece of white card stock; cut a 3¹/₂"x5" piece of green card stock. Center and glue the white piece on the green piece. Adhere a stripe sticker across the top of the card, then sew a whimsical button at the top left corner. Write the poem from the Snowman Soup recipe on page 85 on the recipe card and tuck it in the mug.

129

# GENERAL INSTRUCTIONS

## CROCHET

### ABBREVIATIONS

| | |
|---|---|
| CC | Contrasting Color |
| ch(s) | chain(s) |
| cm | centimeters |
| dc | double crochet(s) |
| FPdc | Front Post double crochet(s) |
| hdc | half double crochet(s) |
| MC | Main Color |
| mm | millimeters |
| sc | single crochet(s) |
| st(s) | stitch(es) |
| tr | treble crochet(s) |
| YO | yarn over |

★ — work instructions following ★ as many **more** times as indicated in addition to the first time.

( ) or [ ] — work enclosed instructions **as many** times as specified by the number immediately following **or** work all enclosed instructions in the stitch or space indicated **or** contains explanatory remarks.

### GAUGE

Exact gauge is **essential** for proper fit. Before beginning your project, made the sample swatch given in the individual instructions in the yarn and hook specified. After completing the swatch, measure it, counting your stitches and rows or rounds carefully. If your swatch is larger or smaller than specified, **make another, changing hook size to get the correct gauge**. Keep trying until you find the size hook that will give you the specified gauge. Once proper gauge is obtained, measure project approximately every 3" (7.5 cm) to be sure gauge remains consistent.

### HOW TO MEASURE CHILD'S HEAD

Measure around crown for head measurement (Fig. 1).

**Fig. 1**

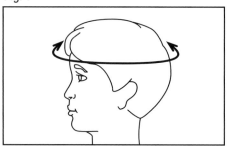

### JOINING WITH SC

When instructed to join with sc, begin with a slip knot on hook. Insert hook in stitch or space indicated, YO and pull up a loop, YO and draw through both loops on hook.

### JOINING WITH HDC

When instructed to join with hdc, begin with a slip knot on hook. YO, holding loop on hook, insert hook in stitch or space indicated, YO and pull up a loop (3 loops on hook), YO and draw through all 3 loops on hook.

### JOINING WITH DC

When instructed to join with dc, begin with a slip knot on hook. YO, holding loop on hook, insert hook in stitch or space indicated, YO and pull up a loop (3 loops on hook), (YO and draw through 2 loops on hook) twice.

### BACK LOOP ONLY

Work only in loop(s) indicated by arrow.

**Fig. 2**

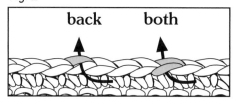

### BACK RIDGE

Work only in loops indicated by arrows.

**Fig. 3**

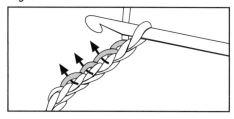

### FREE LOOPS

When instructed to work in free loops of a chain, work in loop indicated by arrow.

**Fig. 4**

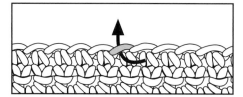

### FRINGE

Cut a 5"x12" piece of cardboard. Wind the yarn loosely and evenly lengthwise around the cardboard until the card is filled, then cut across one end; repeat as needed.

Hold together as many strands as specified in individual instructions; fold in half.

With wrong side facing and using a crochet hook, draw the folded end up through a space or row and pull the loose ends through the folded end (Fig. 5a & 5c); draw the knot up tightly (Fig. 5b & 5d). Repeat, spacing as specified in individual instructions.

Lay flat on a hard surface and trim the ends.

**Fig. 5a**

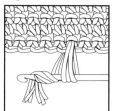

**Fig. 5b**

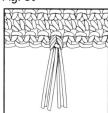

**Fig. 5c**

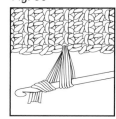

**Fig. 5d**

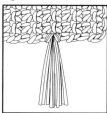

## MAKING APPLIQUÉS

**To prevent darker fabrics from showing through,** white or light-colored fabrics may need to be lined with fusible interfacing before being fused.

**To make reverse appliqués, trace the pattern onto tracing paper;** turn traced paper over and continue to follow all steps using the reversed pattern.

**1.** Trace the pattern onto paper side of fusible web as many times as indicated in instructions. When making more than one appliqué, leave at least 1" between shapes.

**2.** Cutting ¹/₂" outside drawn shape, cut out web shape. Fuse to wrong side of fabric.

**3.** Cut out the appliqué shape along the drawn lines. Remove paper backing.

## COFFEE OR TEA DYEING

**Coffee Dyeing:** Dissolve 2 tablespoons of instant coffee in 2 cups of hot water; allow to cool.

**Tea Dyeing:** Steep one tea bag in 2 cups of hot water; allow to cool.

**For Both:** Immerse fabric or lace into coffee or tea. Soak until desired color is achieved. Remove from coffee or tea and allow to dry. Press if desired.

## CROSS STITCH

**Counted Cross Stitch (X):** Work one Cross Stitch to correspond to each colored square in chart. For horizontal rows, work stitches in two journeys.

**Fig. 1**

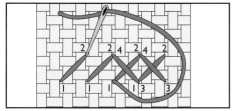

For vertical rows, complete stitch as shown.

**Fig. 2**

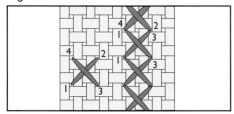

**Backstitch (B'ST):** For outline detail, Backstitch (shown in chart and color key by black or colored straight lines) should be worked after all Cross Stitch has been completed.

**Fig. 3**

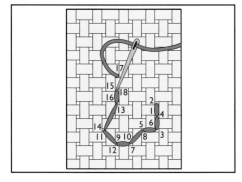

**French Knot:** Referring to Fig. 4, bring needle up at 1. Wrap floss once around needle and insert needle at 2, holding end of floss with non-stitching fingers.

**Fig. 4**

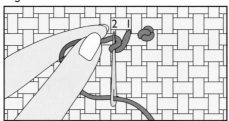

**Quarter Stitch:** Quarter Stitches are shown as triangular shapes of color in chart and color key. Come up at 1, then split fabric thread to take needle down at 2.

**Fig. 5**

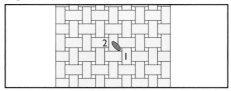

## MAKING PATTERNS

**When the entire pattern is shown,** place tracing paper over the pattern and draw over lines. For a more durable pattern, use a permanent marker to draw over pattern on stencil plastic.

**When patterns are stacked or over-lapped,** place tracing paper over the pattern and follow a single colored line to trace the pattern. Repeat to trace each pattern separately onto tracing paper.

**When tracing a two-part pattern,** draw over the first part of the pattern onto tracing paper, then match the dashed lines and arrows and trace the second part of pattern onto tracing paper.

**When only half of the pattern is shown** (indicated by a solid blue line on pattern), fold the tracing paper in half. Place the fold along the solid blue line and trace pattern half; turn folded paper over and draw over the traced lines on the remaining side. Unfold the pattern; cut out.

## PAINTING TECHNIQUES

**Transferring a pattern:** Trace pattern onto tracing paper. Place transfer paper coated side down between project and traced pattern. Use removable tape to secure pattern to project. Use a pencil to draw over outlines of design (press lightly to avoid smudges and heavy lines that are difficult to cover). If necessary, use a soft eraser to remove any smudges.

**Painting base coats:** Use a medium round brush for large areas and a small round brush for small areas. Do not overload brush. Allowing to dry between coats, apply several thin coats of paint as needed for desired coverage.

**Transferring details:** To transfer detail lines to design, reposition pattern and transfer paper over painted base coats and use a pencil to lightly draw over detail lines of design.

**Adding details:** Use permanent marker or paint pen to draw over detail lines.

**Dry brush:** Do not dip brush in water. Dip a stipple brush or old paintbrush in paint; wipe most of the paint off onto a dry paper towel. Lightly rub the brush across the area to receive color. Repeat as needed.

**Shading and highlighting:** Dip one corner of a flat brush in water; blot on a paper towel. Dip dry corner of brush into paint. Stroke brush back and forth on palette until there is a gradual change from paint to water in each brush stroke. Stroke loaded side of brush along detail line on project, pulling brush toward you and turning project if necessary. For shading, side load brush with a darker color of paint. For highlighting, side load brush with a lighter color of paint.

**Spatter painting:** Dip the bristle tips of a dry toothbrush into paint, blot on a paper towel to remove excess, then pull thumb across bristles to spatter paint on project.

**Sponge painting:** Use an assembly-line method when making several sponge-painted projects. Place project on a covered work surface. Practice sponge-painting technique on scrap paper until desired look is achieved. Paint projects with first color and allow to dry before moving to next color. Use a clean sponge for each additional color.

For allover designs, dip a dampened sponge piece into paint; remove excess paint on a paper towel. Use a light stamping motion to paint item.

For painting with sponge shapes, dip a dampened sponge shape into paint; remove excess paint on a paper towel. Lightly press sponge shape onto project. Carefully lift sponge. For a reverse design, turn sponge shape over.

## MAKING A TAG OR LABEL

For a quick & easy tag or label, photocopy or trace (use transfer paper to transfer design) a copyright-free design onto card stock…or just cut a shape from card stock.

Color tag with colored pencils, crayons, or thinned acrylic paint; draw over transferred lines using permanent markers or paint pens. Use straight-edge or decorative-edge craft scissors to cut out tag; glue to colored or decorative paper or card stock, then cut tag out, leaving a border around it.

Use a pen or marker to write a message on the tag. You can also choose items from a wide variety of self-adhesive stickers, borders or frames; rubber stamps and inkpads; or gel pens in an assortment of colors, densities and point-widths, to further embellish your tags or labels.

## LETTERING

For unique and personal labels or lettering on your crafts, try using one of your favorite fonts from your computer…try the "bold" and "italic" buttons for different variations of the font. Size your words to fit your project, then print them out.

Using your printout as the pattern, use transfer paper to transfer the words to your project. If you're making appliqué letters, you'll need to draw the letters in reverse, then trace them onto the paper side of fusible web.

Don't forget about the old-reliable lettering stencils…they're easy to use and come in a wide variety of styles and sizes. And, if you're already into memory page making, you probably have an alphabet set or 2 of rubber letter stamps…just select an inkpad type suitable for your project. Then, there are 100's of sizes, colors and shapes of sticker and rub-on letters…small, fat, shiny, flat, puffy, velvety, slick, smooth, rough…oh well, you get the idea! Only your imagination limits you.

## EMBROIDERY STITCHES

**Preparing floss:** If your project will be laundered, soak floss in a mixture of one cup water and one tablespoon vinegar for a few minutes and allow to dry before using to prevent colors from bleeding or fading.

**Backstitch:** Referring to Fig. 1, bring needle up at 1; go down at 2; bring up at 3 and pull through. For next stitch, insert needle at 1; bring up at 4 and pull through.

Fig. 1

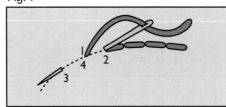

**Blanket Stitch:** Referring to Fig. 2a, bring needle up at 1. Keeping thread below point of needle, go down at 2 and come up at 3. Continue working as shown in Fig. 2b.

Fig. 2a          Fig. 2b

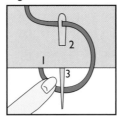 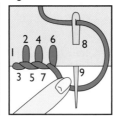

**Couched Stitch:** Referring to Fig. 3, bring needle up at 1 and go down at 2, following line to be couched. Work tiny stitches over thread to secure.

Fig. 3

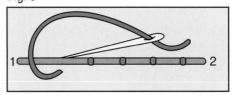

**Cross Stitch:** Bring needle up at 1 and go down at 2. Come up at 3 and go down at 4.

Fig. 4

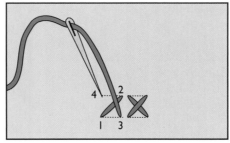

**French Knot:** Referring to Fig. 5, bring needle up at 1. Wrap floss once around needle and insert needle at 2, holding end of floss with non-stitching fingers.

Fig. 5

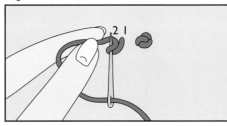

**Running Stitch:** Referring to Fig. 6, make a series of straight stitches with stitch length equal to the space between stitches.

Fig. 6

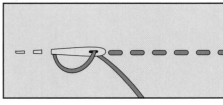

**Straight Stitch:** Referring to Fig. 7, come up at 1 and go down at 2.

Fig. 7

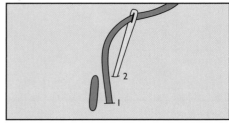

**Whip Stitch:** With right sides of folded fabric edges together, bring needle up at 1; take thread around edge of fabric and bring needle up at 2. Continue stitching along edge of fabric.

Fig. 8

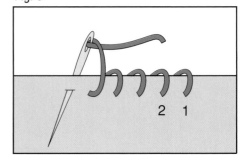

FLANNEL STOCKINGS
(pages 16 and 17)

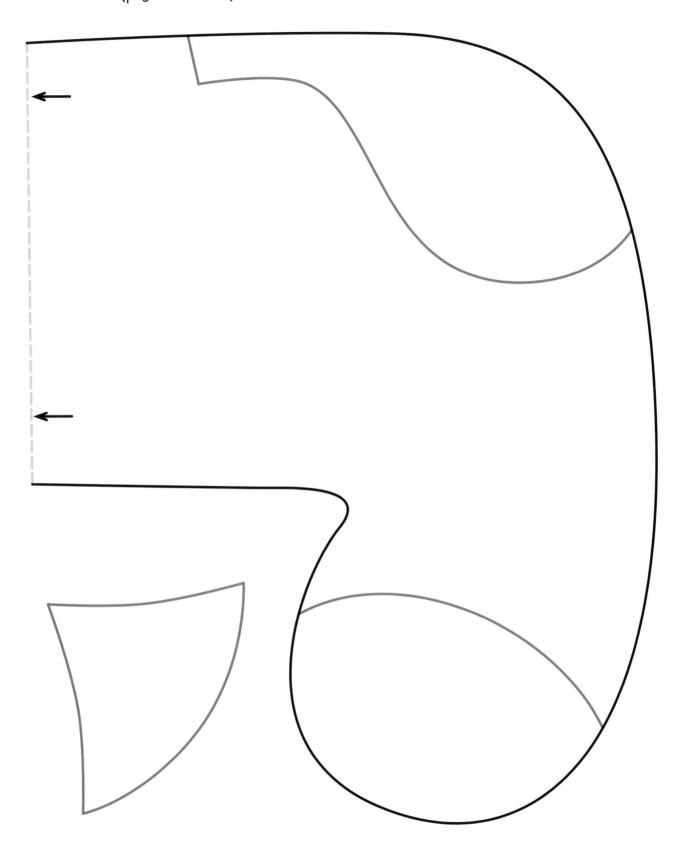

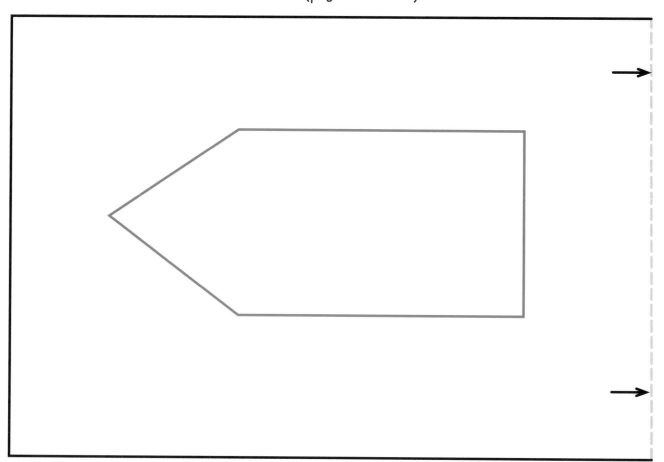

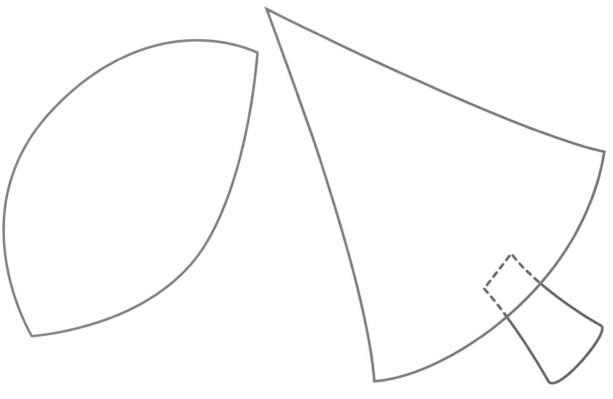

## ANGEL ORNAMENT
### (page 22)

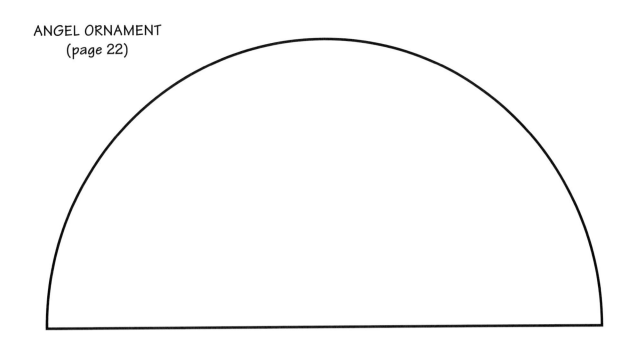

## "LET IT SNOW" SIGN
### (page 24)

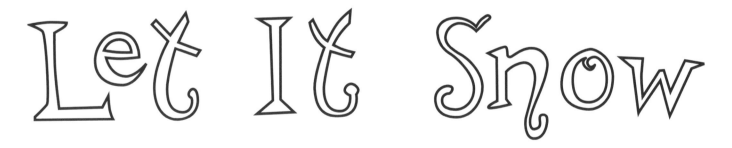

# SNOWMAN DRAFT STOPPER
## (pages 26 and 27)
enlarge 125%

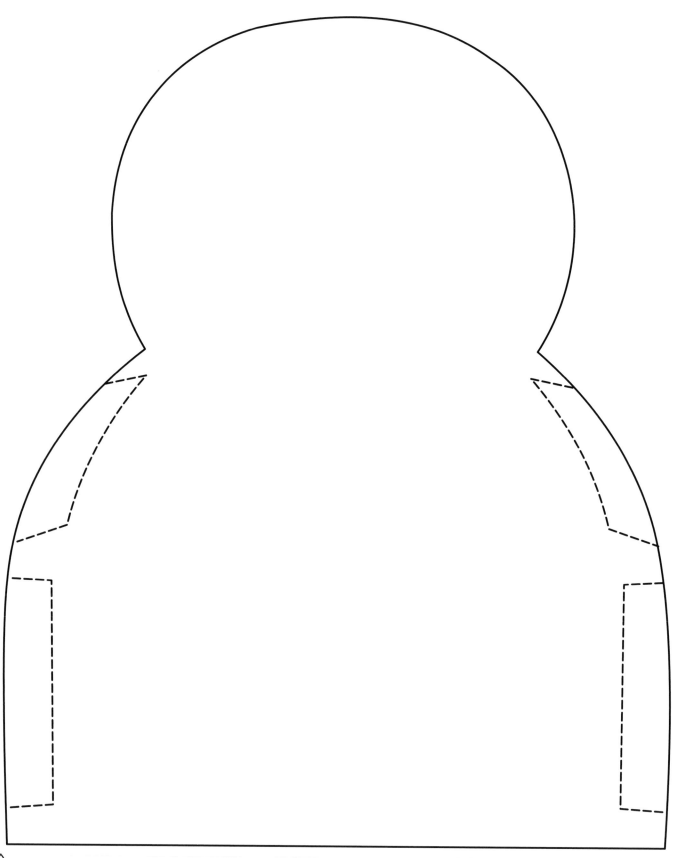

136

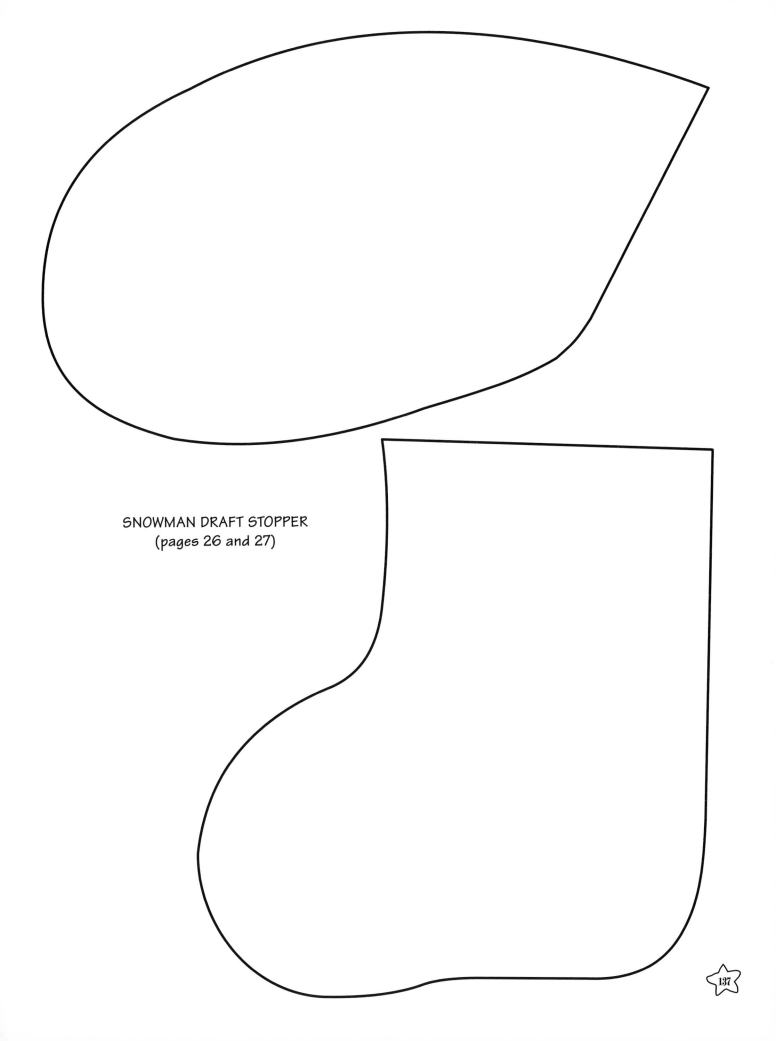

SNOWMAN DRAFT STOPPER
(pages 26 and 27)

137

STUFFED SNOWMAN
(page 23)

SNOWMAN PORTRAIT
(page 25)

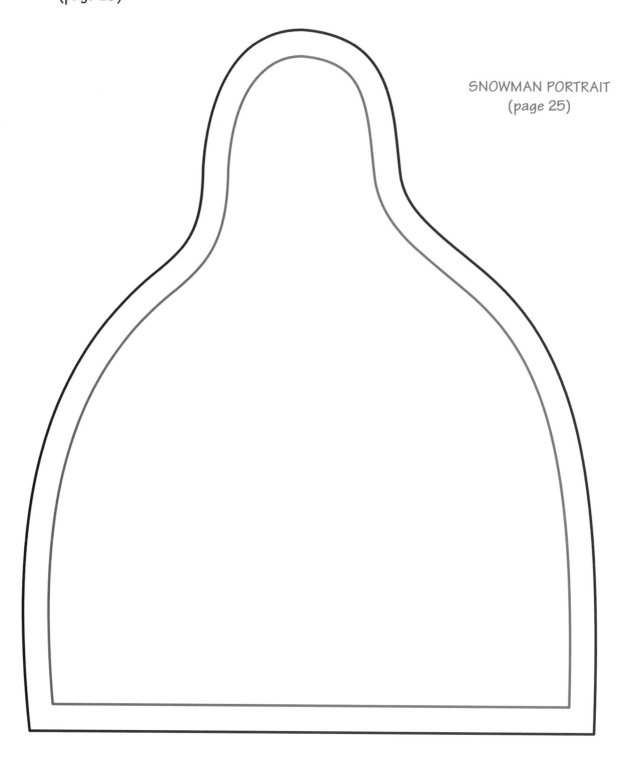

FELT ORNAMENTS
(pages 30 and 31)

139

# PAINTED PLATE
## (page 32)

# ETCHED PLATE & GLASS
## (page 37)

## STITCHED SANTA AND TEDDY COLOR CHART
### (page 40)

| X | DMC | 1/4X | B'ST |
|---|-----|------|------|
| · | blanc | | |
| ◄ | 310 | | ⟍ |
| ∟ | 350 | ⟍ | ⟍ |
| ⊗ | 352 | ⌐ | |
| ○ | 353 | ○ | |
| ✱ | 400 | ⟍ | |
| ⊞ | 435 | ⊞ | |

| X | DMC | 1/4X | B'ST |
|---|-----|------|------|
| 6 | 436 | 6 | |
| + | 437 | + | |
| ▶ | 552 | ◣ | |
| ◆ | 699 | ◥ | ⟍ |
| 4 | 702 | 4 | |
| − | 712 | − | |
| m | 721 | m | |

| X | DMC | 1/4X | B'ST |
|---|-----|------|------|
| | 727 | | |
| ∣ | 738 | ! | |
| n | 813 | ◢ | |
| $ | 817 | ◣ | ⟍ |
| | 825 | | |
| ∷ | 951 | ∷ | |
| ⌐ | 3033 | ⌐ | |

| X | DMC | 1/4X |
|---|-----|------|
| ◁ | 3326 | ◁ |
| ⊘ | 3608 | ⊘ |
| ▽ | 3743 | ▽ |
| 2 | 3812 | 2 |
| ● | blanc french knot | |
| ○ | 727 french knot | |

STITCHED SANTA AND TEDDY

(page 40)

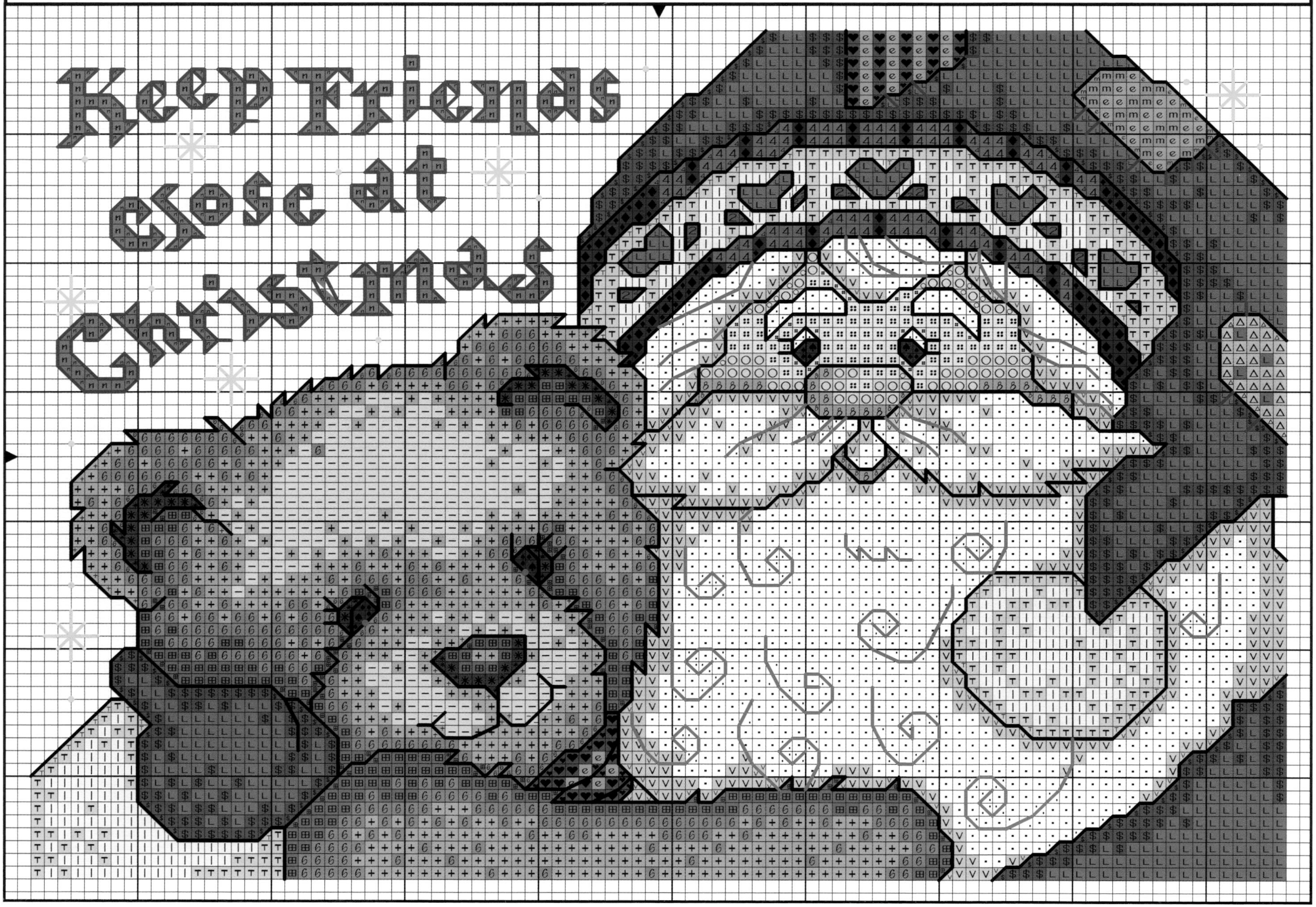

# CANDLE BANDS
## (page 41)

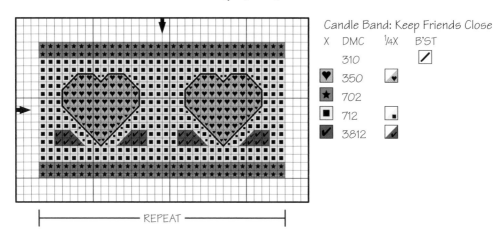

Candle Band: Keep Friends Close

| X | DMC | ¼X | B'ST |
|---|-----|-----|------|
| | 310 | | / |
| ♥ | 350 | | |
| ★ | 702 | | |
| ■ | 712 | | |
| ✔ | 3812 | | |

REPEAT

# CHILD'S APRON
## (page 52)

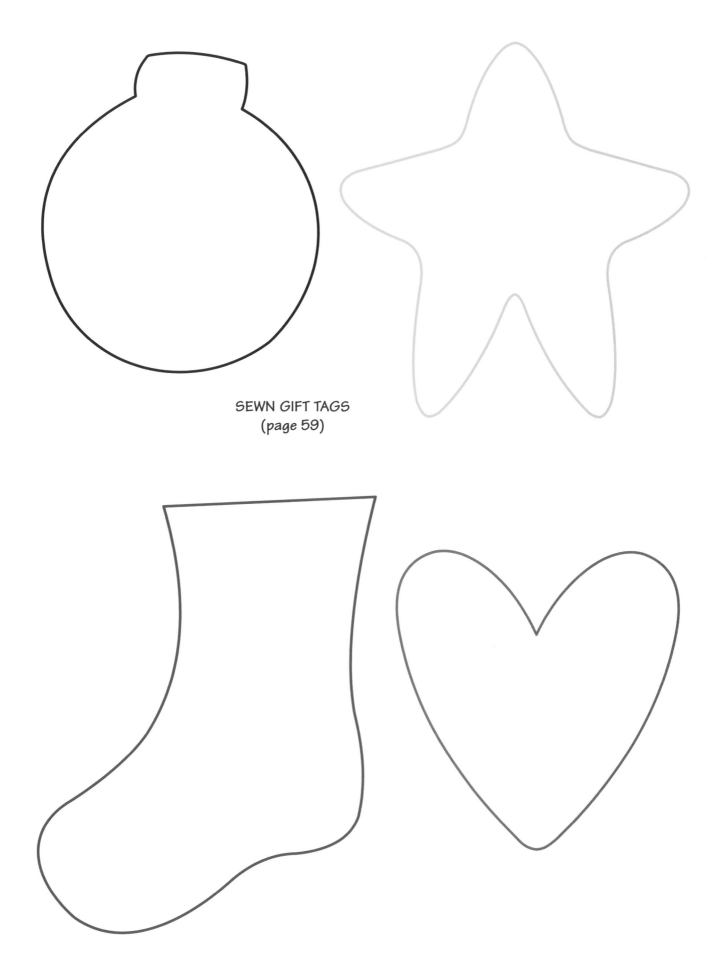

SEWN GIFT TAGS
(page 59)

# PENNY RUG TREE

**TREE TOPPER**
(page 42)

**TREE SKIRT**
(page 43)

**MANTEL SCARF**
(pages 44 and 45)

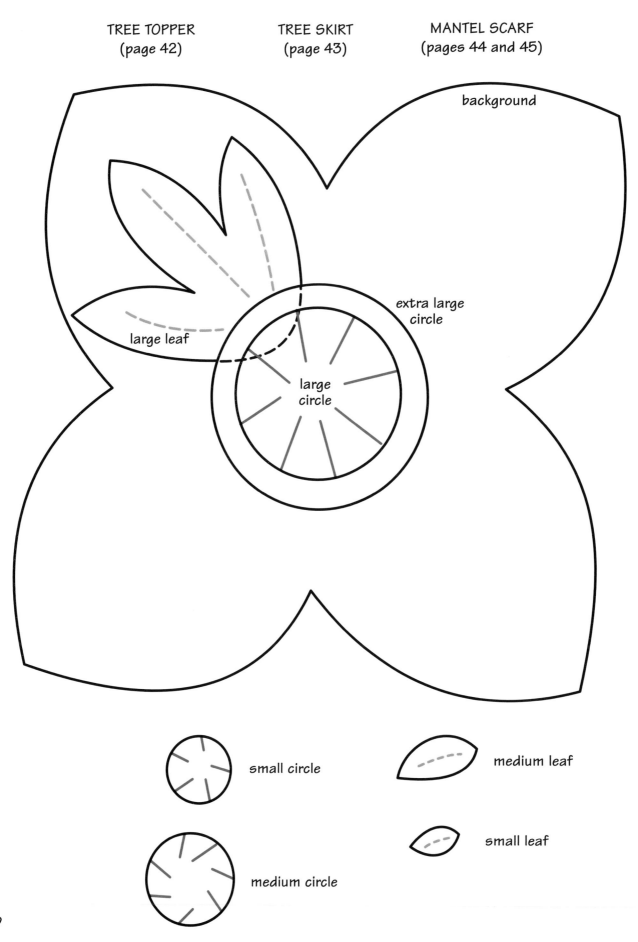

background

large leaf

extra large
circle

large
circle

small circle

medium leaf

small leaf

medium circle

144

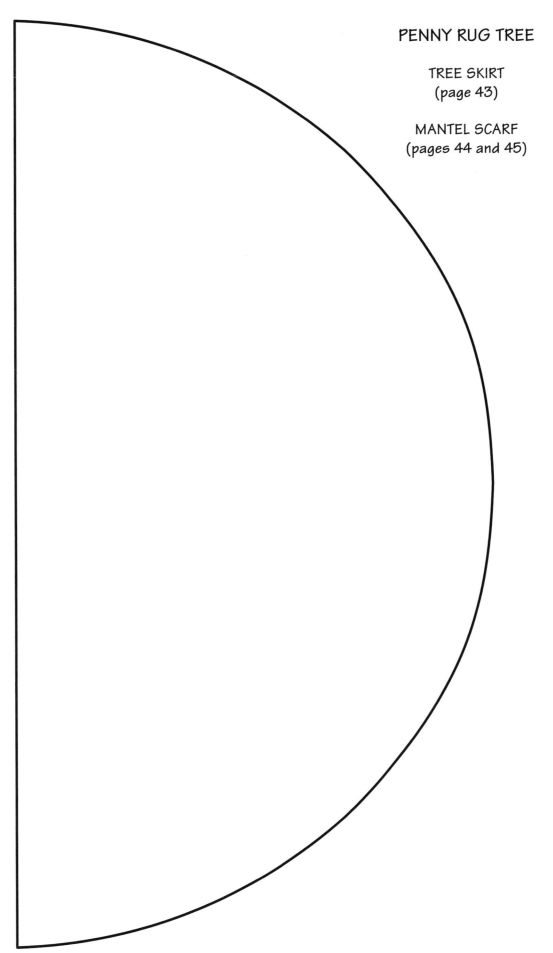

PENNY RUG TREE

TREE SKIRT
(page 43)

MANTEL SCARF
(pages 44 and 45)

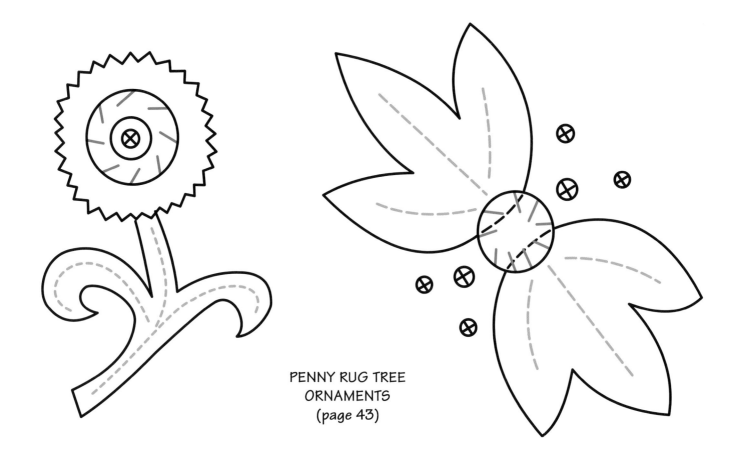

PENNY RUG TREE
ORNAMENTS
(page 43)

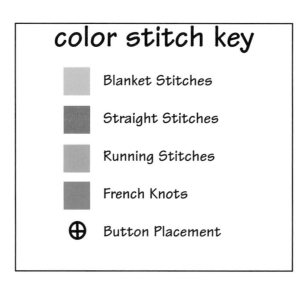

## color stitch key

Blanket Stitches

Straight Stitches

Running Stitches

French Knots

⊕ Button Placement

PENNY RUG TREE
ORNAMENTS
(page 43)

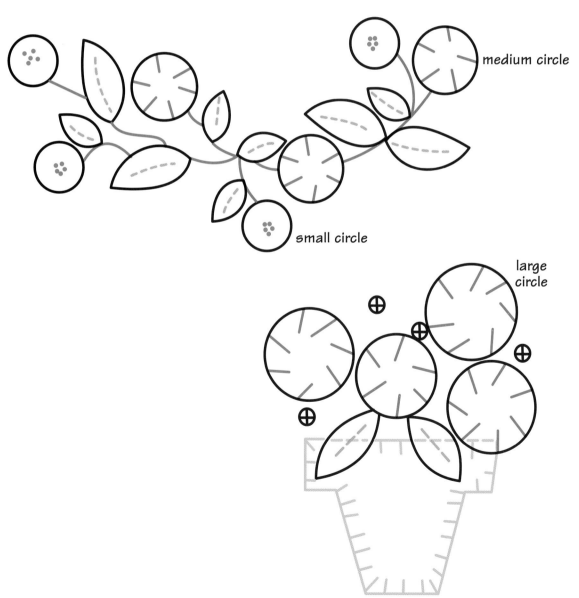

medium circle

small circle

large
circle

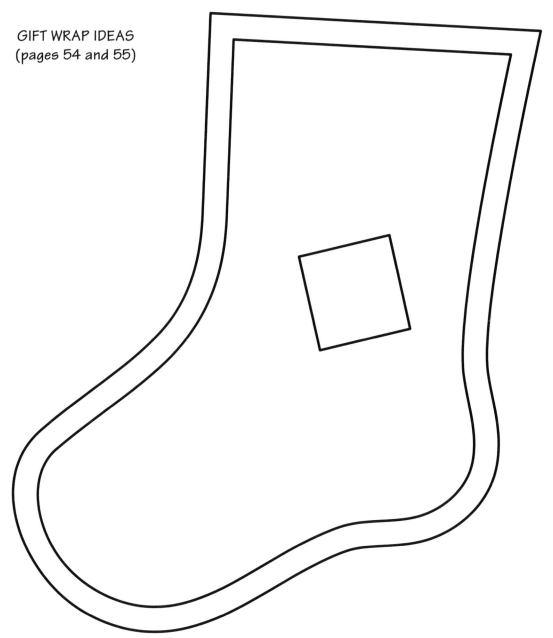

GIFT WRAP IDEAS
(pages 54 and 55)

APPLIQUÉD SNOWMAN
SWEATER
(page 64)

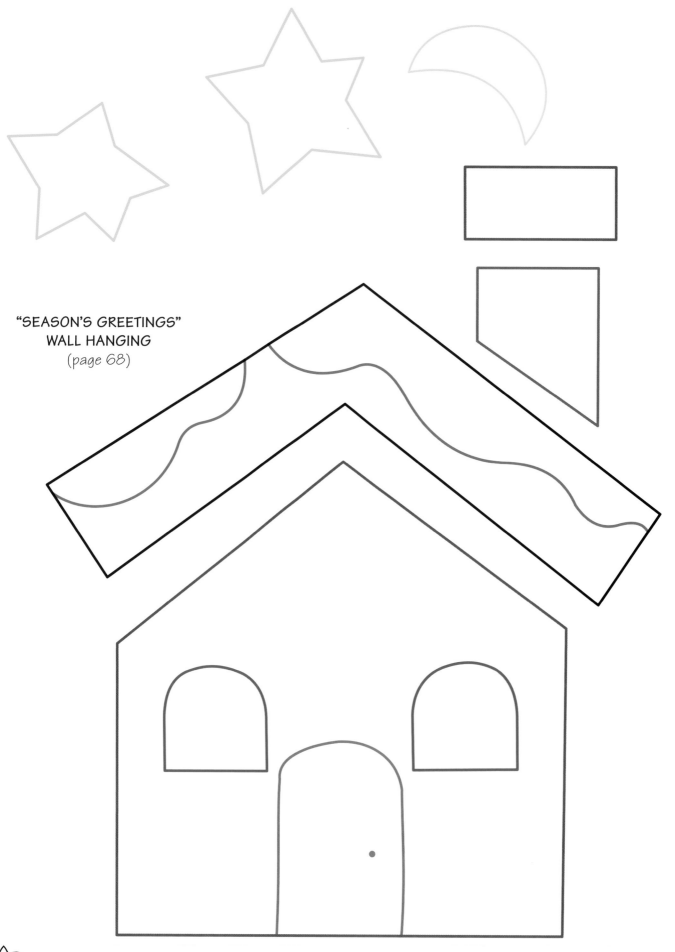

"SEASON'S GREETINGS"
WALL HANGING
(page 68)

Season's Greetings

"SEASON'S GREETINGS"
WALL HANGING
*(page 68)*

151

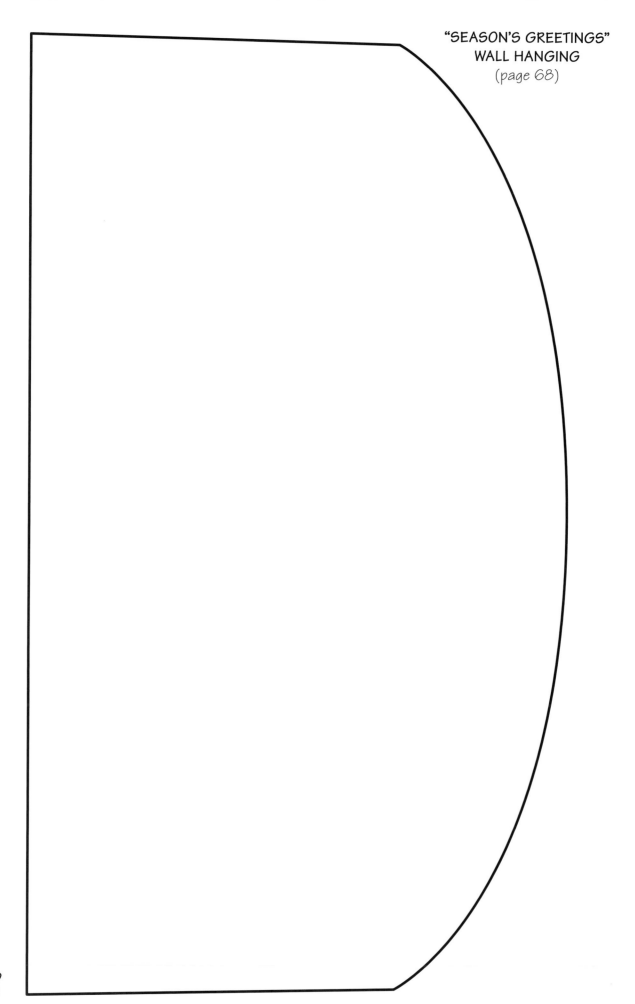

**"SEASON'S GREETINGS"
WALL HANGING**
*(page 68)*

153

# SNOWMAN PLATE

*(page 75)*

## MUFFIN MIX TAG

(page 83)

Pour mix in large mixing bowl and make a well in center of dry ingredients. Beat together one egg, 1/3 cup oil, one cup shredded sharp cheddar cheese & one cup milk. Combine with mix; stir to moisten. Fill 12 greased muffin cups 3/4 full. Bake at 400 degrees for 15 to 20 minutes. Cool 5 minutes, then remove from muffin tins. Makes one dozen muffins.

Snow* flake Muffin Mix

## BROWNIE MIX TAG

(page 81)

from our Holiday House to yours

coconut Brownie Mix

merry christmas from

## TEA MIX TAG
### (page 82)

## LITTLE HANDS TAG
### (page 84)

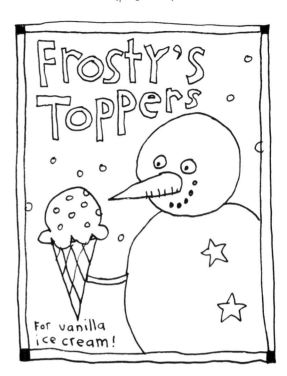

## LITTLE HANDS TAG
### (page 84)

## LITTLE HANDS TAG
### (page 84)

# Italian Pasta Fagiola Soup

recipe:

2 T. olive oil
1 carrot, chopped
1 stalk celery, chopped
½ lb. ham, cubed

2 · 28 oz. cans Italian plum tomatoes, chopped
4 c. chicken stock or water
Pkg. bean & spice mix
pasta

In a large soup pot, sauté carrot, celery & ham in olive oil. Add tomatoes, chicken stock or water and bean mix. Bring to a boil. Cover partially, reduce heat & simmer 2 to 3 hours 'til beans are tender. Pasta may be added now. Cook about 5 to 7 minutes or 'til pasta is al dente. (You may prefer to cook pasta separately, place in bottom of bowls and then spoon hot soup over the pasta.) Garnish with finely shredded Parmesan cheese.

from the little elves in the _____ kitchen:

# North · Pole · Cookie · Bars

Combine jar mix with ½ cup melted butter, one egg and one teaspoon vanilla extract; blend well. Press cookie mix in a greased 8" baking dish ∽ bake at 350 degrees for 18 to 22 minutes or until golden and almost set. Makes 16 bars ∽ enough for you and your little elves!

# PROJECT INDEX

# RECIPE INDEX

# Credits

We wish to extend warm thanks to those people who allowed us to photograph some of our projects at their homes, especially Joan, Walter, Beth, Bonnie, Steph, Lyn, Tabby, Alison, Fae, Bonnie and Don, Robert, Jane, Sue, and Judy, the owner.

The metal candlesticks shown on page 56 and the copper tops that are shown on pages 58 and 60 purchased from our gallery stock product shops, which is there are good work visible from our gallery stock. Some of the individual, contemporary craftsmen. We wish to acknowledge that all of these are in their creativity, and it may do well with the wood public art, for some. Once, Gary, with ....

We wish to thank our talented photographers, Gary R. Davis of Davis Davis Photography, Andrew Kilgore studio of Andrew Kilgore Photography, and Mark Madison and Ben West of The Stephen group, all Madison Park, gallery at our gallery for their work. Photographs stylist, Sandra Gabbe, Mary Ann Whitney, Scott, and Carol Wilson. We express our appreciation for the high quality of their talents and care in the photography.

We express a special word of thanks to the following designers: Susan Sheppard who designed the model rooms at Trader development of designer, and the David Phelps in craftsman and gallery ... Eric and Anne Baxter, who designed the individual work and craft designer, the ... Mark Gilman, who designed the sketch for this, that Sandra Gabbe design for Susan Jackson who designed the side, presented as exhibitions for many of the individual, who had the designer's works, craftsmen, with their work, on works in the works.

We would like to acknowledge the other companies for providing some of the materials and tools used to make our projects: Design Master Color Tool, Inc. and ... Nu-Foil Colorado (spray tools and accessories, etc.); National Art Materials company, Skokie, New York City; and Husqvarna/Viking The Sewing Machine Company of Cleveland, Ohio (Sewing machines).